Peace-ing It Together

Peace and Justice Activities for Youth

Pat Fellers

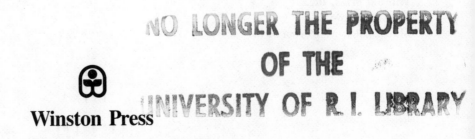

Winston Press

To
Al and Annette Fellers
My first teachers on
peace and justice

Cover design: Nancy Condon

Book design: Reg Sandland

ISBN: 0-86683-836-8

Printed in the United States of America

5 4 3 2 1

Winston Press, Inc.
430 Oak Grove
Minneapolis, Minnesota 55403

ACKNOWLEDGEMENTS

The following must be thanked for making this book possible:

- Sr. Patricia Baxter, SNJM and Sr. Barbara Collier, SNJM who shared their visions of peace and supported this project from the very beginning.
- Christie Maddocks and Karen Meyer for their help with the lettering.
- Anne Marie Eltagonde for helping with the children's book list.
- Debi Lake for her typing skills.
- Jim Sheridan and his staff at Chapels who helped with resources.
- Kathy Gritzmacher and Molly Chun for their support and many ideas.
- Amy, Jeani, and Molly for helping me to realize why peace education is so important.
- Al and Annette Fellers, Debi and John Lake, Marilyn and Tom Fink for having the time to help me.
- Audrey DeLaMartre for editing this manuscript and sharing her good ideas.
- Dolores Ready and Susan Weinlick of Winston Press for believing that peace education is important.
- Staff, students, and families of Holy Redeemer School for their ability to be "Rainbow People" and make education for peace and justice a daily reality.

TABLE OF CONTENTS

What Is Peace Education?

Welcome to the World of Peace Education.

For twelve years I have worked on a peace and justice curriculum for elementary classrooms. First, I worked out individual units. Then, in 1975, a special Peace Committee created Bicentennial Peace Packets. Three years of the monthly newsletter *Peace-ing It Together* culminated in this text which is a composite of all preceding projects.

Peace education isn't new. It has always been found in classrooms that encourage positive self concepts, community, nonviolent conflict resolution, and a global perspective to world problems. However, if a peace education program is to be effective, it must be more than a catchy theme for a school year or a thirty minute lesson in November. Peace education is a philosophy, a way of life, part of every subject and activity.

Peace education is:
• Creating a positive self-image
• Building a spirit of community
• Being aware of world problems
• Recognizing global plurality and interdependence
• Action! Determining our role

Peace education begins with adults who realize that children need models of Christian values more than critics. They need:
• Adults who know how to live in community
• Adults who have developed a meaningful relationship with God
• Adults who express their feelings
• Adults with a growing faith
• Adults who solve problems nonviolently
• Adults who view themselves as world citizens
• Adults who recognize and preserve the gifts of the earth
• Adults who celebrate Jesus as the Prince of Peace
• Adults who live the promise of the Resurrection.

Thus, the key to this peace program is the teacher. Respect can't be taught until it's experienced. Community can't be built until it's lived. Peace and justice concepts can't be taught in a classroom where management is a constant concern. Teaching "one earth, one family" is impossible in a classroom where there is a history of unresolved conflict.

The future presents many challenges. Each day wars are fought, thousands die of starvation, and nuclear destruction threatens. The realities of the 80's offer us few options. Our children must be taught to live effectively with these realities. We have one home, planet Earth, and what happens to one happens to all.

We must believe that peace is possible during the 1980s. And we must teach peace to reach peace. We hope this text will help you promote a peaceful classroom environment and infuse your curriculum with peace and justice concepts.

World peace does not have to be a dream. Peace is possible and peace education must become a classroom priority.

Welcome to the world of peace education.

Starting Right

This chapter explores ways we can teach peace by creating a positive self concept and building a spirit of community in our classrooms.

We've been given the gift of a year to make a difference in the lives of those we teach. The activities in Chapter One can help make that difference.

Dear God . . .

We have been given the gift of another year to create, to love, to grow. What we do with our gift of time is up to us:

We can fill our curriculum plans with vitality and life, or we can do just enough to get by.

We can accept the challenges offered of creating an environment of love each day, or we can make excuses and say our class is not ready for such risk-taking.

We can make a conscious effort to grow in faith, love, and trust, or we can think of school as a place to spend time.

We have been given the gift of time:

A whole year to make a difference in the lives of other people.

A whole year to grow in our own faith.

A whole year to teach as Jesus did.

A whole year to make peace and justice a reality.

Thank you, God, for this gift. Help us to use it wisely, and to remember that this gift of time will not be ours again. Amen.

Sound Familiar?

Joanne Peterson teaches the sixth grade in a Portland school. When she joined the faculty three years ago, she was excited about her job. In her initial interview she heard about the Christian values that were not only part of the curriculum, but were also part of the working atmosphere. Joanne believed that in this environment, she could make a difference.

Throughout her first year Joanne waited to see these values in action. She had supposed the other teachers valued cooperation, nonviolence, and multi- cultural education. However, school rules and policies were discussed in terms of specifics, not in terms of human dignity. The problem of world hunger was talked about at Thanksgiving, and then only in vague terms. When a teacher told about a family in need, sympathy was expressed but no action followed. Joanne soon learned that Christian values and the school's philosophy were subjects covered only in the principal's interview. Unfortunately, school personnel were not committed to living the philosophy.

Joanne Peterson doesn't exist, but her situation does. Schools must begin positively and live their Christian philosophy. We must be convinced that every person has the right to dignity.

Where Do I Start?

During the first nine weeks, we are offered an opportunity to build the foundation for a successful school year. The blueprint can include plans for student management, recognizing and appreciating individual personalities, and problem solving.

You may wonder what this has to do with peace education. It has everything to do with it! Education for peace and justice means creating positive self esteem, living and learning in an environment that recognizes the importance and dignity of each person, and building a spirit of community that includes the many parts of a school family. Peace education begins in everyday life. Students learn to relate to a world community by experiencing a sense of belonging in their own classrooms. They learn to discuss alternatives to war by learning to solve problems in nonviolent ways. They learn to respect the dignity of others by understanding that their own lives have merit and worth.

The first term offers the challenge of building the foundation for a successful program in peace and justice.

Building Staff Relationships

We all spend many hours building positive relationships in the classroom, yet we often overlook building good staff relationships. We offer many excuses: there's too much to do in our classroom; there isn't enough time;

we're too tired to take on anything else. While each excuse has merit, we must take a long, hard look at the picture our school staff presents to those we teach. If they see a fragmented staff, little sharing or caring, limited working for common goals, they will wonder about our commitment to building community. Peace and justice education starts with the staff. (Notice the emphasis on staff rather than just teachers. If we are saying to the students that each of them is important to the group and they see us leaving out other school personnel, we imply that community is selective.) We must unite if this Pilgrim Church on Earth is to follow the example set by Jesus and go together to God.

One way to build staff relationships is to present the idea of each staff member sharing a talent. All staff members will write their special talent to share during September on a symbol which can be displayed on a wall. All may design their own symbol or all might use the same symbol. A symbol of the sun like the one below might be used.

The symbol should be large enough that the staff can write their talents and other necessary details. For example:

- "My talent is art. I will share a fall art project with those interested." Time: Place:
- "My talent is baking. I will bake two loaves of bread to share with the staff at lunch."
- "My talent is sports. I will plan a sports night for the staff."

Not all staff members will be able to take advantage of all the talents. Those on diets won't eat the bread, yet they can still appreciate the skill used in making it.

Maybe you won't choose to attend the sports night, but you can be grateful for someone providing the opportunity.

Be vocal, tell others you appreciate their talents. Write an affirming comment on their symbol when it's displayed. Give them your support.

The staff should review school policies together, discuss guidelines for duties, and write procedures in justice terms. Example:

- We will share our gifts and talents with one another because a community depends on sharing.
- We will include all adults in our staff community because students must see that community is not selective.
- We will be at our classroom door when class begins because each student has the right to be greeted by name.

When the guidelines are complete, have a volunteer type them and ask all the participants to sign the paper. Give each staff person a copy and post one in the staff room.

Ask Yourself

- Do I maintain fair, understandable, and consistent goals in the classroom and not demand too much one day and too little the next?
- Do I keep an open mind about my students' abilities?
- Do I manage to bring smiles to the faces of all my students?
- Do I give my students enough time to exchange ideas, thoughts, and feelings?
- Do I maintain a peaceful atmostphere in the classroom?
- Do I recognize the dignity of each student and treat each with respect?

Things to Do

It is important for our students to feel that each of them is important. We can share this message in a variety of ways with students. The following activities help to lay the foundation for a peaceful classroom by building self-respect and a sense of responsibility.

The Magic Mirror.
Put a mirror in a small box. Tell your students that in the box you have the most important person in the world. There will be lots of guesses, but then have each student look in the box. Caution them not to tell the answer until all have had a turn. Good tool for discussion, "What gifts do I have to offer the world?" Also, a great way to tell students once again, "You are special." Older students like this activity, too.

Roll Call Interviews
A good way to start the day with class involvement is to ask the students an interview question during the roll call. Everyone begins the day with the opportunity to appreciate individuality and the teacher knows who is present. (Please see Activity 4.)

Sample questions:

- What is the best place you ever visited?
- What is your favorite color?
- What is one nice thing about yourself?
- How many members are in your family?
- What part of the newspaper do you read first?
- What does your family do together?
- What chores do you do around the house?
- Where were you born?
- What is your favorite food for lunch?
- What is your favorite book?
- What time do you go to bed?
- What time do you get up?
- What present would you give your mother for her birthday?
- Who is your favorite recording artist?
- What is your favorite number?
- What is your favorite TV show?

Reporter of the Week
Each week one class member records significant accomplishments, special events, and curriculum highlights. At a designated time, the student reporter shares with the class and a short period of evaluation could follow. For example:

- Billy's grandmother died in Boston.
- This week we participated in a Friendship Assembly by singing our class song, "Rainbow People."
- Margaret won an award from the Fire Safety Contest.
- Liz won $10.00 for her Traffic Safety poster.
- Danny's dog was hit by a car.
- Mr. Davis came in to give us a compliment about our behavior in the hall.

These weekly pages can be put into a booklet and saved week after week. (Please see Activity 10.)

Time Capsules
Space limitations may dictate personal capsules or a class capsule. This activity could be completed the first week of school with the capsule opened during the last week of school.

The discussion could begin with this question: How have we changed since the time capsule was put together?

Grandparents Day
On this day in September the students could draw their family tree. Perhaps the tree could be incorporated into a card. Discuss how life has changed since their

grandparents were in school.

Birthday Book
Each student will research what happened on the day they were born. They may consult an almanac or other reference materials. Students will put their research in a booklet and then on their birthday share their findings with the class. Current headlines can then be added. Students can draw conclusions about how life has changed through the years. (Please see Activity 11.)

Tracing
Students trace the *outline of their hand.* Cut out outlines and then arrange them from the smallest to the largest. Display them on a bulletin board or around the classroom. Discuss what the outlines show about physical changes that are yet to take place.

Stories of the Future
Make an *imaginary trip* to a school of the 21st century on its opening day. A creative story might include:

• How do students get to school?
• Where is the school located?
• What classes do they take?
• What do they do for homework?
• What sports do they play?
• What is the biggest problem facing the school?

Classroom Yellow Pages
This activity encourages students to reflect on their special talents and hobbies and to share them with the classroom community. Students will list curriculum strong points, special interests, hobbies, languages, athletic activities, etc. Once individual pages are complete, the pages can be put together to complete the "Classroom Yellow Pages." (Please see Activity 12.)

A Get Well Message
When students are ill and absent for more than a few days, make them a "Get Well Puzzle." Have the students write a short message in the center of a piece of posterboard, then have all the class members sign the card. Other school personnel may also be asked for their autographs. Complete the decoration and then cut the board into puzzle pieces. Put the pieces in a decorated envelope and have a class member deliver the special get well message.

Student of the Week

Since it is often easy for us to overlook a quiet or shy student, or fail to take time to look for the good in a disruptive student, Student of the Week offers us an opportunity. During the first week of school, put each student's name in a box. Draw out the names of the students and assign them a calendar week. It is easier if

you have a calendar right there and write the names on the week.

Students plan and create their own bulletin board using the chalk board or a large piece of poster board. The student brings baby pictures, family pictures, and holiday snapshots, as well as special awards.

Student of the Week hands out and collects papers, or may run errands and deliver messages.

Students will complete a special page for each Student of the Week. (Please see Activity 1.)

Rules

Our students need to take part in planning the rules that govern them. During the first day of school, have students define a few guidelines that will help them live peacefully together. Examples:

• "We will be friendly and polite to everyone in our class since we all have the right to be treated with dignity."
• "We will work quietly because we don't have the right to disturb others."

When rules are completed, have each student write them as a special assignment. Print a special copy for the bulletin board and have every class member sign it. (Please see Activity 6.)

Sharing Talents

During the first week of school, have the students think of a talent they can share with the group during September. After they think it over they will make a symbol of sharing and write their talent to share on it. Display the symbols in the classroom. Have the symbols large enough so comments can be written after the talent is shared. Encourage the students to explore themselves and to think about how they relate to the people around them. (Please see Activities 2, 3, and 12.)

Feelings

Children need to recognize and acknowledge feelings. To be aware of others' feelings, we must be aware of our own. Here are some activities that help explore the area of feelings. (Please see Activities 5 and 7.)

Have the students write a poem describing themselves. For example:

	Title
First line:	Noun describing yourself
Second line:	Two adjectives describing yourself
Third line:	Three words telling what you like to do
Fourth line:	Phrase telling about yourself
Fifth line:	Your name

Gather pictures of people of all ages engaged in many different kinds of activities. Then make a list of different kinds of feelings:

frustrated	lonely	important	mad
excited	proud	depressed	content
upset	jealous	puzzled	anxious
uncomfortable	tense	angry	disappointed
happy	satisfied	concerned	pleased
worried	terrific	shocked	

Match each picture with a feeling. Create a bulletin board with your pictures and feeling words.

Mask Passing

One person puts an unusual expression on his or her face. He/she then passes it on to the next person. This continues until everyone in the circle has received and given a facial expression.

Giant Heart

Another possibility is to make a giant class heart. Each person draws a name out of a hat and writes one positive thing about that person. All of the cards are then put into the class heart.

Group Cooperation Drawing

The whole class draws a scene, for example, a block on the street, or the school. Each person draws one thing that fits proportionately with the rest of the drawing. After it is completed, the whole class looks at the work and discusses it.

Listening to Each Other

Students must learn to listen to each other. This classic story produces interesting discussion on the value of listening.

Six Who Looked at an Elephant (A Folk Tale)

Once upon a time, six wise men lived together in a small town. The six wise men were blind.

One day, an elephant was brought to the town. The six men wanted to see the elephant, but how could they?

"I know," said the first man. "We will feel him!"

"Good idea," said the other five. "Then we'll know just what an elephant is like."

So the six men went to see the elephant.

The first one touched the elephant's big, flat ear. He felt it move slowly back and forth. "The elephant is like a fan," the first man cried.

The second man felt of the elephant's legs. "He's like a tree," the man cried.

"You're both wrong," said the third man. "The elephant is like a rope." This man was feeling the elephant's tail.

Just then the fourth man pricked his hand on the elephant's sharp tusk. "The elephant is like a spear," he cried.

"No, no," cried the fifth man. "He's like a high wall." As he spoke, he felt of the elephant's side.

The sixth man was holding the elephant's trunk. "You are all wrong," he said. "The elephant is like a snake."

"No, no, like a rope."

"Snake!"

"Wall!"

"You're wrong!"

"I'm right!"

The six wise men shouted at each other for an hour. And they never found out what an elephant was like.

Questions:

• How did the blind men feel when they heard an elephant was coming?

• Why did each man think the elephant looked a different way?

• Was each man right? Why?

• Was each man wrong? Why?

• How could the story have been different if the wise men had listened to each other?

• Were the men happy at the end of the story? Why?

Rewrite an ending to this story. (Please see Activity 8.)

Sharing With Each Other

The Cookie Game

The first week of school offers time to talk about sharing. This game provokes an interesting discussion and is a popular activity.

Materials: 1 package of cookies; envelopes with numbers sealed inside (one for each student)

Directions: Write "0" on four slips of paper, "3" on four slips, and "1" and "2" on all the rest. Seal each slip in a separate envelope and hand one envelope to each student. One at a time, the students stand and open their envelopes and read aloud the number on the slip of paper. If the number is two, the student gets two cookies, if the number is three, the student gets three cookies, but if the number is zero, the student doesn't get any. The same procedure is followed until everyone has had a turn.

After the game ask the following questions:

1. Will all the people who got three cookies please come forward? How did you feel when you saw the "3" and then received three cookies?

2. Now will all the students who received a "0" in their envelope come forward? How did you feel when you saw your "0"? How did you feel when you watched all your classmates receive and eat their cookies? Do you like this game? Why?

3. Did any of you share with your classmates who received less than you? What does the word sharing

mean? How are we going to share in our classroom?

You might want to discuss that some people did not understand that not everyone got the same number of cookies. Were they surprised? Did they know what to do? (Please see Activity 9.)

After the discussion, please make sure that those students who received a zero get some cookies.

Note: In the many times I have played this game with students, I have *never* had a group actually share with one another. I usually time this game to be played just before lunch and, without an exception, when the students see their number and get their cookies, they pop them into their mouths. After the sharing discussion they always ask if they can play the game again because now they know how to do it. I stress that in some way we will play the game every day all year.

Also, I put a little star on the back of all the envelopes with a "3" inside and a little plus sign on those with a "0" inside. While it may seem a little stacked, I would never give a "0" to a shy student. Instead I usually give it to a self assured student who easily vocalizes feelings and would not be crushed by not getting any cookies.

Learning About Friendship

Play a song about friendship (piano, record, cassette) to introduce a discussion on friendship. Then divide the class into small groups and hand out one of the following quotations to each group.

- "The only way to have a friend is to be one."
- "All for one and one for all."
- "Friendship is the only cement that will hold the world together."
- "A friend is a gift you give yourself."
- "Friendship doubles your joy and divides your grief."
- "I get by with a little help from my friends."
- "There are no strangers, only friends we haven't met yet."
- "On the path between homes of friends grass doesn't grow."
- "A friend in need is a friend indeed."

The students will discuss the meaning of their assigned quotation and then share their findings with the classroom community. Older students may research the source of each quote in a book of quotations.

Students then fill out a Friendship Survey. (Please see Activity 13.) The student pages could be compiled in a booklet and put in the classroom library so students can share ideas.

To continue thinking about friendship, students can complete the sentence, "For my friend I would . . . ." (Please see Activity 14.)

Students could write a "Recipe For a Friend." What ingredients would be included in the recipe? (Please see

Activity 15.) Students will share their recipe with other class members.

For a summary, students can complete several sentences describing a good friend. (Please see Activity 16.)

Good Books About Friendship

PRESCHOOL AND PRIMARY GRADES

Amigo, Byrd Baylor Schweitzer (Collier).
A little Mexican boy and a prairie dog find and love each other.

Ask Mr. Bear, Marjorie Flack (Collier).
When a little boy hunts for just the right birthday present for his mother, kindly Mr. Bear has the right answer, a gift that costs nothing but comes from the heart.

A Birthday For Francis, Russell Hoban (Scholastic).
As her little sister Gloria's birthday approaches, Frances wavers between being generous and being jealous.

Crow Boy, Taro Yashima (Viking).
A shy Japanese boy is recognized and accepted by his classmates through his teacher's understanding and sympathy.

Fiona's Bee, Beverly Keller (Dell Yearling).
Fiona had no friends. She finds a bee and decides to take her pet to the park for a snack. On the way Fiona becomes famous. A lonely girl finds an unusual friend.

Frederick, Leo Lionni (Pantheon).
Frederick, the mouse, makes a unique contribution to the winter survival of his friends by feeding their depressed spirits with beautiful thoughts and visions.

Frog and Toad Are Friends, Arnold Lobel (Scholastic).
Frog and Toad's adventures are filled with the give-and-take of friendship.

The Happy Lion, Louise Fatio (Scholastic).
A lion in a zoo discovers the sad truth about his friends.

The Hating Book, Charlotte Zotolow (Harper and Row).
A close friendship almost falls apart because of a misunderstanding. This book points out the responsibility of each person in a relationship to say how he or she is feeling.

Harvey's Hideout, Russell Hoban (Scholastic).
Two argumentative muskrats, brother and sister, discover that it is more fun to share and be friends than to brood alone and be enemies.

Ira Sleeps Over, Bernard Weber (Houghton Mifflin).
Ira struggles to decide whether or not to take his teddy bear when he goes to spend the night at a friend's house.

Letter to Amy, Ezra Keats (Harper and Row).
A boy decides to chance the ridicule of his friends by inviting a girl to his birthday party.

Let's Be Enemies, Janice Udry (Scholastic).
John goes to tell James that they are enemies, but they remain friends.

Little Brute Family, Russell Hoban (Collier).
Five disagreeable Brutes are happily transformed as one little good feeling changes the lives of all.

The Little Fox in the Middle, Pearl S. Buck (Collier).
The middle cub of a fox family finds an unexpected friend in a little boy.

The Little Red Hen, Paul Galdone (Seabury).
A little red hen teaches three lazy friends an important lesson.

Mean Max, John Peterson (Scholastic).
Eight-year-old Tony learns the meanings of friendship, fear, pride, and love.

The Midnight Fox, Betsy Byars (Viking).
Tom, not an outdoor type at all, reluctantly stays with his aunt and uncle in the country. His rescue and subsequent friendship with a black fox make a memorable summer.

A Mouse to Be Free, Joyce Warren (Camelot).
A small brown mouse is befriended by a young girl who learns what love really means when the mouse is ready to return to the world.

The Quarreling Book, Charlotte Zolotow (Harper and Row).
One person's bad mood makes the next person angry. Soon the entire family is making nasty comments until someone breaks the spiral.

Stevie, John Steptoe (Harper and Row).
Although Stevie is a pest, when he moves away Robert misses him and appreciates the good times they had together.

Swimmy, Leo Lionni (Random House).
The small red fish are afraid to go anywhere because the big fish will eat them. Swimmy organizes them to swim together to look like the big fish.

That's What Friends Are For, Florence Heide (Scholastic).
The elephant's friends learn that friends help.

Will I Have a Friend?, Miriam Cohen (Collier).
The reassuring story of a milestone in every child's life, the first day of school.

INTERMEDIATE GRADES

The Bears' House, Marilyn Sachs (Yearling).
Everyone in Fran Ellen's class knows her name. They know that she sucks her thumb and smells bad. But they don't really know anything important about her. They don't know that she lives in two houses. One is with her brother and sisters and sick mother. The other house is the Bears' house. Most of the kids think it is only a doll's house, but for Fran Ellen it is real. A tragic story about the need to love and to be loved in return.

Beady Bear, Don Freeman (Viking).
A loveable toy bear leaves his happy home to live in a cave, but Beady Bear finds out what he really needs to be happy: friendship.

Benny the Misfit, Hila Colman (Scholastic).
Benny takes the bus to an inner city school. As he learns to adapt, his parents change too.

The Big Wave, Pearl S. Buck (Scholastic).
Jiya and Kino, two Japanese boys, live and work together on a farm, learning that living in the presence of danger can make a person brave and teach him to appreciate life.

The Blind Connemara, C. W. Anderson (Collier).
A young girl's patience and understanding help a courageous blind pony to victory.

Bully of Barkham Street, Mary Stolz (Harper and Row).
Marvin finally realizes that he creates his own problems and becomes happier when he begins to change.

Charlotte's Web, E. B. White (Dell Yearling).
A beautiful gray spider lives in the barn with her friend Wilbur the pig. Charlotte teaches Wilbur the meaning of friendship.

The Cricket in Times Square, George Seldon (Dell).
A cricket from Connecticut spends a summer in New York City and finds three wonderful friends.

Ellen Tibbits, Beverly Cleary (Scholastic).
Ellen and her best friend have a disagreement and then make up.

Fanshen, the Magic Bear, Becky Sarah (New Seed Press).
After talking to the Magic Bear, Laura convinces the people to stop cooperating with the oppressive king.

Harriet the Spy, Louise Fitzhugh (Dell).
A hilarious, often touching story of an independent,

curious, and totally honest girl who has the misfortune of having her secret notebook found by her classmates.

Higher Than the Arrow, Judy Van Der Veer (Scholastic).
Lucy is lost in a blizzard. Frances sent her home by a shortcut that leads straight into the wilderness. She did it because she was jealous and angry and wanted to get rid of Lucy. Frances feels awful, but there's nothing she can do.

Iggie's House, Judy Blume (Dell Yearling).
The Garber family moved into Iggie's house. The Garbers are black; Grove Street is white and always has been. Winnie, a welcoming committee of one, sets out to make a good impression and be a good neighbor. That's how all the trouble starts.

Lizzie Lies a Lot, Elizabeth Levy (Dell Yearling).
Lizzie tells lies. This convincing story explores how Lizzie learns to accept her own successes and limitations and solves her lying problem.

Mary Jane, Dorothy Sterling (Scholastic).
While caring for an injured squirrel, a lonely black girl finds a friend at a newly integrated junior high school.

Meaning Well, Sheila Cole (Dell Yearling).
A sensitive look at the effects of peer pressure. Lisa is torn between what she knows is right and acceptance by her best friends.

Member of the Gang, Barbara Rinkoff (Scholastic).
Bored and tired of being criticized by his parents, Woodie joins a street gang. He soon realizes that his goals and his family's goals differ greatly from those of the other Scorpions.

Otherwise Known as Sheila the Great, Judy Blume (Dell).
Sheila Tubman is afraid of dogs, spiders, the dark, and thunder. She can't swim or work a yo-yo. Sheila learns to overcome her fears by admitting them.

The Peppersalt Land, Marilyn Harris (Scholastic).
Two 12-year-old girls, one black, one white, are confronted with the ugliness of racism in a small southern community.

A Pocketful of Cricket, Rebecca Caudill (Holt).
A young farm boy, with a deep affection for the beautiful sights and sounds of the world around him, allows his classmates to share his very special, private world.

A Private Matter, Kathryn Ewing (Scholastic).
Marcy was so hoping to have a friend next door. Her mother works and her schoolmates don't live nearby. A retired couple moves in and she knows she has found a friend in Mr. Endicott. He's someone who is always

there, who's easy to talk to, almost like a father. This is a story of a friendship so special that Marcy calls it "a private matter."

Queenie Peavy, Robert Burch (Viking).
Queenie is thirteen, her father is in jail and Georgia is in the grip of the Depression, but Queenie learns to make the most of what she has.

Ready-made Family, Francis Murphy (Scholastic).
Three lonely orphans must adjust to new foster parents.

Roosevelt Grady, Louisa Shotwell (Scholastic).
A nine-year-old black boy is determined to learn so that he can be free from slave-like conditions.

The Secret Garden, Frances Burnett (Dell).
A girl discovers that life is exciting, that she likes herself and living. She finds a way to share these new discoveries with her invalid cousin.

Sensible Kate, Doris Gates (Viking).
While trying to be sensible, a plain little orphan girl learns that it is not necessary to be beautiful to be loved.

The Shy Little Girl, Phyllis Krasilovsky (Houghton Mifflin).
Shy Anne, who lives in a nice house with a nice mother and father, gradually gathers self-confidence and begins to learn the fun of friendship and sharing.

Sidewalk Story, Sharon Bell Mathis (Avon).
Tanya is being evicted with her mother and her six brothers and sisters. Their furniture and belongings will be piled on the sidewalk and left for anyone to take. It doesn't matter if no one else in the entire city cares, Lilly Etta does, and she won't let it happen. This is a story about Lilly Etta, a story about Tanya, it is a story about friendship.

Susan and Sereena and the Cats Place, Nan Agle (Scholastic).
A young girl who is having difficulty growing up and coping with her parents' divorce learns to understand her own problems through friendship with an eccentric old woman.

The Were Fox, Elizabeth Coatsworth (Collier).
A boy and an imaginary creature have a compellingly real friendship.

A White Heron, Sarah Orne Jewett (Crowell).
A girl must decide whether or not to show her friend, the hunter, the nest of her favorite bird. This story points out moral choices that people must make.

A Wrinkle In Time, Madeleine L'Engle (Dell).
Meg travels through outer space to find her father. She

also has a delightful friendship with her mother who is a scientist.

UPPER GRADES

About the 'Bnai Bagels, E. L. Konigsburg (Aladdin).
The summer Mark's mother became manager of his Little League team and his best friend moved away brought more problems than any boy ought to endure.

Best Friend, Shirley Simon (Archway).
Many girls will identify with Jenny and her best friend problem which is handled with a light, sure touch in this lively tale.

The Boy Who Could Make Himself Disappear, Kin Platt (Dell).
Roger Baxter, new and lonely in New York, has a speech impediment and a tough time making friends.

Durango Street, Frank Bonham (Dell).
As a black boy struggles against gang life in a ghetto, a youth worker seeks to help him.

Guy Lenny, Harry Mazer (Dell).
Guy, twelve years old, is in a lot of trouble that is not his fault, enough trouble to make a fellow want to run away.

I Was a 98 Pound Duckling, Jean Van Leeuwen (Dell).
Because being thirteen can be something of a disaster, teenagers will identify with Kathy's lack of self-confidence, fear of rejection, and daydreaming.

Look Through My Window, Jean Little (Harper).
Emily moves into an eighteen room house and five wild cousins are coming to stay. Emily discovers that sharing herself and possessions is very rewarding, if sometimes exasperating. Best of all, Emily discovers the joys of friendship.

The Pigman, Paul Zindel (Dell).
Two lonely high school students and a strange old man find unexpected love and laughter with each other, until the unreal world they create is shattered and the young people are left to confront the harsh realities of their lives.

The Soul Brothers and Sister Lou, Kristin Hunter (Avon).
A young girl gains new awareness of her own worth and pride in her black heritage.

Student of the Week

By_____

I THINK YOU ARE
TALENTED AT:

_____

_____

_____

_____

THE THING I LIKE BEST
ABOUT YOU IS:

_____

_____

_____

_____

DEAR_____

_____

_____

_____

_____

FROM _____

I BELIEVE THAT YOU ARE

LOVING_____ KIND_____
CLEVER_____ FUNNY_____
SWEET_____ GIVING_____

PLEASE CHECK AT LEAST 2.

YOU SHOW THAT YOU
UNDERSTAND WHAT IT MEANS
TO BE A CHRISTIAN WHEN YOU:

_____

_____

_____

_____

People, People Who Need People

By _____

Name five people who love you.

_____

_____

_____

_____

_____

Name four people who go out of their way for you.

_____

_____

_____

_____

Name four people who have learned something from you.

_____

_____

_____

_____

Name three people you admire.

_____

_____

_____

Name five people who give you compliments.

_____

_____

_____

_____

_____

Name three people who are patient with you.

_____

_____

_____

Name four people who make you feel important.

_____

_____

_____

_____

Thinking It Over

By _____

My biggest success so far is _____

_____

Three things I do very well are _____

_____

_____

_____

My biggest failure so far is _____

_____

Something I've done that helped promote peace _____

_____

Someone in my life that I'm very proud of is _____

because _____

Something I did that took courage is _____

_____

I look forward to the future because _____

_____

_____

Special Awards

By _____

If you could award prizes, who would you honor in the following categories?

Most Important Person in History:_____

Best Bible Story:_____

Best Song:_____

Best Restaurant in the World:_____

Peacemaker of the Year:_____

Best Month of the Year:_____

Best Book Ever Written:_____

Best Day of the Week:_____

Best Television Program:_____

Favorite President:_____

Most Beautiful Place in the World:

_____

Person of the Year:

_____

Meaningful Descriptions

By _____

I am: _____

_____

_____

My school is: _____

_____

_____

My family is: _____

_____

_____

Men are: _____

_____

_____

Women are: _____

_____

_____

Americans are: _____

_____

_____

Russians are: _____

_____

_____

Native Americans are: _____

_____

_____

Our Classroom Rules

By _____

These are our classroom rules for the school year

1. _____
   _____

2. _____
   _____

3. _____
   _____

4. _____
   _____

5. _____
   _____

6. _____
   _____

7. _____
   _____

Communicating Through Feelings

By _____

How do you show happiness? _____

_____

How do you show anger? _____

_____

How can you tell when a person
is angry? _____

_____

How do you show anxiety? _____

_____

How do you show boredom? _____

_____

How can you tell when someone
else is bored? _____

_____

How do you show disappointment? ___

_____

How can you tell when someone else
is disappointed? _____

Reflections on "Six Who Looked at an Elephant"

By _____

1. What lesson did this story teach you? _____
_____

2. Why didn't the blind men listen to each other? _____
_____

3. Why is listening to other people important? _____
_____

4. What are three things you should remember when listening to someone else?
_____
_____
_____

5. Listening is _____

6. Retell the story in your own words. _____
_____
_____
_____
_____

Reflections on the Cookie Game

By _____

1. How many cookies did you receive? _____

2. How did you feel? _____
_____

3. When did Jesus share with others? _____
_____
_____
_____

4. What did Jesus tell us about sharing? _____
_____

5. What does the word *sharing* mean? _____
_____

6. How are you going to share with others this school year?
_____
_____
_____

7. How do you want others to share with you? _____
_____
_____

8. Sharing is _____
_____
_____
_____

A Special Week

Reported By _____

Date _____

Special Events

Shared Sadness

Headlines in the News

What We're Learning in School

Humerous Happenings

My Birthday Book

By _____

My Birthday Is _____

Important Events that Happened on that Day

Other People Born on My Birthday

Birthday Wishes

Current Headlines

Classroom Yellow Pages

By _____

My Name _____ Date _____

Hobbies

My Special Talents

Important People I Know

I'm an Expert in

Friendship Survey

By _____

My Name _____ Date _____

Are you a good friend to someone? _____

Who? _____

Have you ever lost a friend? _____

Why? _____

Have you ever tried to be friends with someone no one else likes? _____

When? _____

Have you ever tried to be friends with someone who didn't like you? _____

When? _____

Is it hard to stay angry when a friend says, "I'm sorry"? _____

Why? _____

Can a friend do something bad and still be your friend? _____

Why? _____

Do you have a best friend? _____

Who? _____

Are you friends with yourself? _____

How? _____

For My Friend I Would

By _____

1. If my friend fell down on the playground, I would _____
_____

2. If my friend ripped my spelling paper by accident, I would _____
_____

3. If my friend needed five cents for a class fieldtrip, I would _____
_____

4. If my friend took a toy from a story, I would _____
_____

5. If my friend promised to go to the movies and then didn't, I would ____
_____

7. If my friend was being cruel to an animal, I would _____
_____

8. If my friend forgot her or his lunch, I would _____
_____

9. If my friend wanted to copy my science test, I would _____
_____

A Recipe for Friendship

By _____

"Friendship doubles your joy and divides your grief."

Start with . . .

Add . . .

Blend in . . .

Combine . . .

Frost with . . .

My friend is _____

Key Words:

understanding	sympathy	patience
tolerance	companionship	sense of humor
generosity	helpfulness	honesty
appreciation	acceptance	gentleness

Share your recipe with a friend.

Thinking About a Friend

By _____

My friend's name is _____

I met my friend _____

The thing I like best about my friend is _____

_____

The thing I like least about my friend is _____

_____

My friend's favorite game is _____

My friend's favorite TV show is _____

My friend's favorite food is _____

My friend's favorite color is _____

My friend is really good at _____

My friend's family is _____

My friend's favorite school subject is _____

Are you surprised at how much or how little you know about your friend? Why?

_____

Why is it important to know about a person for that person to be a good friend?

_____

_____

CHAPTER TWO

Peaceful Procedures

Chapter Two examines three procedures that can help make your classroom more peaceful and organized. Peaceful Procedures includes "Classroom Self-Managers," "Consequences," and "Peaceful Lines."

Dear God . . .
You have blessed me with many special talents. With your help I can do many things well. I live in a world filled with injustice. I see war, suffering, hatred, and evil every day. Help me to have the courage to face the wrongs.

Give me the hope to know that with your love I can make a difference.

Help me to see the pain of fear and loneliness, and to know that I can offer a smile and word of kindness and find a new friend.

Help me to develop a lifestyle of simple living and to know that with a joyful heart I can offer my sacrifices to you.

Help me to learn to respect the earth and to know that its resources are a gift from you.

Help me to look beyond my own community, to realize my responsibilities to my sisters and brothers in the world, and to know that together we are the People of God.

Help me to look again at the manger scene and to know that I am a part of that continuing story.

Slow me Down, God.

Help me to see that I can work for justice.

Help me to follow the example of your Son, Jesus.

Convince me that I can and must make a difference.

Send your Holy Spirit to renew my courage.

May I appreciate the dignity of the people in my family, congregation, and neighborhood.

Help me to see that a person shouldn't be used or manipulated, but must be nurtured by the family and society.

Show me how to be part of the nurturing process.

Dear Lord,

Help me to be a Christian. Amen.

Students as Self-Managers

Step One

Sidney Simon has said it so well, "I am lovable and capable" in his book *I Am Lovable and Capable* (Argus Communications). (Please see Activity 17.)

Print letters *IALAC* (pronounced (I-ah-lack) in large letters on a sheet of paper. Tell the class, "Everyone wears an IALAC sign. You can't see it, of course, but it's still there, and it's impossible to remove. The letters stand for some very important words: I AM LOVABLE AND CAPABLE. Everyone carries an invisible IALAC sign around with them at all times and wherever they go. The size of our sign, or how good we feel about ourselves, is often affected by how others interact with us. If someone is nasty to us, teases us, puts us down, hits us, then a piece of our IALAC sign is destroyed." Illustrate by tearing off a piece of your sign.

Then tell a story about a boy or girl who is the same age they are. A sample story might include:

• Getting up late
• Not finding the right clothes
• Missing the bus
• Forgetting homework
• A name calling incident
• Being picked last for a game
• Falling down
• Getting a bad grade
• Dropping a tray in the lunchroom

As you describe each event that negatively affects the student's IALAC sign, tear off another piece of the sign until by the end you are left with almost nothing.

At the end of the story discuss:

• How does your IALAC sign get torn apart?
• What things affect you the most?
• What do you do that destroys the IALAC sign of others in school or at home?
• How do you feel when your IALAC sign is torn?
• When you tear someone else's?
• What can we do to help people enlarge their signs rather than make them smaller?

Step Two

Now that we are more aware of our own feelings, as well as others', we look around the classroom environment to discover problem areas. The three main ones usually are: talking, completing assignments, listening/ following directions. The students each get a sheet each day that looks like this:

PRIMARY GRADES:

Name					
Assignments	5	4	3	2	1
Talking	5	4	3	2	1
Directions	5	4	3	2	1

INTERMEDIATE AND UPPER GRADES:

Name										
Assignments	10	9	8	7	6	5	4	3	2	1
Talking	10	9	8	7	6	5	4	3	2	1
Directions	10	9	8	7	6	5	4	3	2	1

Each student starts the day with five or ten, depending on their level. If a student talks or fails to follow directions, you just say quietly, "Cross off one by talking, (or following directions). This frees you from lengthy lectures and nagging. The paper is also a constant reminder to the student.

At the end of the day, evaluate all the papers together and have the students graph their scores on a piece of graph paper. If you don't want to graph all three, do one problem area.

After two weeks you will have a good idea who can manage themselves and who still needs a little assistance. (Please see Activities 18 and 19.)

Step Three

A teacher does not have the time or energy to manage every student in the class (love them and care about them, yes, but manage them, no!). Those students who are consistently scoring nines and tens on their record sheet are your first self-managers. During a class meeting discuss the criteria for managership (completion of assignments, being a good citizen, sharing with others). Continue the discussion now by listing privileges (sitting by a friend, helping to plan class projects, for example). *It is important for each class to determine their own criteria and privileges.*

Once a student becomes a self-manager, he or she receives a sign for his or her desk and a certificate to take home. Start with four or five managers and announce the others as the situation warrants. Some years you might have all self-managers by Christmas. Other years you may still have three or four you are managing in June. But that is the secret: three or four we can deal with, thirty is overwhelming. So, when twenty-five are self-managers, your two or three "problems" don't have anyone to talk or play with, the pressure of group example comes into play, and the results are amazing. This is currently being used at all grade levels successfully.

If a student has a bad day, his self-managership can be held "in trust" for a day or two. It can be earned back. Rarely does it need to be taken away—usually a reminder will do.

Consequences

Students need to know what behavior is expected of them. They also need to take part in planning the rules that govern them. During the first days of school, help the students make a few rules that will encourage everyone to live peacefully together. Once a rule has been suggested and accepted by the class, write the statement in justice terms:

• We will be friendly and polite to everyone in our class since we all have the right to be treated with dignity.
• We will work quietly because we don't have the right to disturb others.
• We will try to do our best on all our assignments because we need to use the talents God gave us.

To help students write a rule in justice terms, simply ask "Why?" after the rule has been stated.

• "We will walk in the halls." *Why?* "So others won't be hurt."

Once rules have been established, it is important that they be followed. What happens when a student continually refuses to obey the rules? What recourse do we have? Staying after school, a grand lecture, or writing from a dictionary are options which produce frustration and anger on both sides. A more realistic alternative is The Consequence Box.

The Consequence Box teaches students that they are responsible for their own behavior. If a student chooses to disregard a class or school rule, consequences must be paid.

How Do You Use the Consequence Box?
First, get a recipe box and some file cards. Number the file cards, write a consequence on each card, and place the cards in the recipe box. Here are examples of consequences you might use.

1. The Beatitudes say, "Blessed are the peacemakers." What is a peacemaker? Write an example of how you have been a peacemaker.
2. List three talents you have developed: How did you use your talents today?
3. What three important things would you tell a friend about Jesus?
4. Think of a person who loves you. Write three sentences about how that person shows they love you.
5. Think of a time you helped a friend. Tell what you did and how you felt.
6. Write three important rules every classroom should have. How do you follow these rules?
7. What does the word "Silence" mean? Why do people need a time of silence in their lives?
8. List three ways you can show respect for others. Write a sentence about how you show respect for others.
9. Christians believe in Jesus. Write three things you believe in.
10. The "Golden Rule" is "do unto others as you would have them do unto you." What does this mean? Write an example of how you follow this rule.
11. In a dictionary look up the meaning of the word "cooperation." How do you live the meaning of "cooperation?"

12. Think of a person you know who does good things for others. Who is this person and what do they do? How would you like to be like that person?
13. If you were a teacher, how would you handle a student who didn't obey the rules? Why?
14. List three ways that bad behavior can separate us from the people we love.
15. Christians take time to be kind to one another. Tell about a time you were kind to someone who wasn't your best friend.
16. Write four things you like about yourself. What do you like best?
17. Write three things you like about your family. What do you like best?
18. Write three things you like about your school. What do you like best?
19. Look up the word "responsibility" in the dictionary. In what ways do you show you are responsible for your own behavior?
20. List three reasons why people might show off. How would you handle a student who had the habit of showing off?
21. Write a short prayer to Jesus thanking him for loving you.
22. List three ways you can handle a disagreement with someone without resorting to hitting.
23. Who is your best friend? Why do you like him or her? Why does she or he like you?
24. Jesus said, "Love one another as I have loved you." How do you show people you love them?
25. Jesus said, "Happy are those who show mercy to others." How have you shown mercy to other people?
26. Jesus said, "Love your enemies and pray for those who mistreat you, so that you will become the sons and daughters of your Father in heaven." Write about a time you were good to someone who was mean to you.

Next, make a supply of Consequence Report forms such as this one.

Consequence Report Form

Name_____ Consequence #_____
Date_____
_____
_____
_____
Teacher's Signature_____

Explain to the students that when the situation arises, they will be asked to take the first consequence card in the box and a Consequence Report form.

The student will then complete the Consequence Report and return it with the index card. You will sign the completed Report and return the consequence to the back of the file box. Students will usually have one day to complete the consequence.

This may sound complicated, but it isn't. When negative behavior occurs, it is calmly acknowledged, the consequence assigned, and behavior can be discussed in a spirit of peace and positive reinforcement.

The Consequence Box helps a student to reflect on positive behavior patterns and frees the teacher from the "Lecture/Tune-out" syndrome. Students are helped to learn to solve problems involving conflict.

Peaceful Lines

Do you have students in your class who watch the clock and race to the door to be first?

Do you have students who push or shove to be first, often at the expense of others?

Do you have students who are always in line?

Would you like an easy solution to these problems? Actually, it's so simple, I don't know why it took me ten years to think of it. Since lines are necessary in most classes, here is a simple, fair solution.

After students have used this process, it can be analyzed to show how rules and agreements can lead to order and a sense of cooperation.

After you have had a chance to get to know the students, assign everyone a place in line.

Assigned places are a good idea because:

- Everyone gets one week to be first in line, one week to be second, third, fourth, and so on, and one week to be last.

- The second in line is door holder for the week, losing their place in line for only one week.

- The last person closes the door, turns off the lights, accepting special responsibility.

- You take special "grouping problems" into consideration when assigning places. This way you don't have to continually separate troublemakers, and you can avoid reinforcing negative self-concepts.

- You have taken the competition out of lining up. Students needn't run or push because they have a special place and no one may take it.

- You have a pre-arrangement for any occasion. When out of the classroom, all you have to say is, "Class, please get in order," and your lines are ready to go.

Reflection: I A L A C

By _____

1. What does I A L A C stand for? _____

_____

2. What happened to your sign today? _____

_____

3. Did you have to tear your sign in pieces? Why? _____

_____

_____

4. How did you feel when your I A L A C sign was torn? _____

_____

5. What do you do that destroys the I A L A C sign of others? At school? At

home? _____

_____

_____

6. What can you do to help other people enlarge their signs rather than make

them smaller? _____

_____

_____

_____

_____

Reflection: Working in a School Setting

By _____

Please rate yourself in the following areas.

	Excellent	Good	Unsatisfactory
Completing class assignments	_____	_____	_____
Using study time	_____	_____	_____
Working neatly	_____	_____	_____
Obeying school rules	_____	_____	_____
Sportsmanship	_____	_____	_____
Listening to directions	_____	_____	_____
Following directions	_____	_____	_____
Working quietly	_____	_____	_____
Respecting others	_____	_____	_____
Managing myself	_____	_____	_____

My behavior in the classroom is_____

_____

I could improve my behavior by_____

_____

How do you plan to become a classroom Self Manager?_____

_____

_____

_____

Managing Yourself

By _____

Name _____ Week of_____

1. STUDY SKILLS	Unsatisfactory	Good	Terrific
a) completed all class assignments	_____	_____	_____
b) used study time well	_____	_____	_____
c) worked independently	_____	_____	_____
d) completed work neatly	_____	_____	_____

2. PERSONAL SKILLS			
a) obeyed school rules	_____	_____	_____
b) good sport (inside & out)	_____	_____	_____
c) courteous to all	_____	_____	_____
d) listened to directions	_____	_____	_____
e) followed directions	_____	_____	_____
f) no excess talking	_____	_____	_____

COMMENTS

Teacher_____

Parent's Signature_____

Comments:

Resolving Conflict

Nonviolent conflict resolution is an essential ingredient of education for peace and justice. It is vital that children learn a process for resolving conflicts. Teachers must teach nonviolent conflict resolution and plan for conflict times.

Chapter Three provides activities centered on the concepts of conflict and peace.

Dear God . . .
We pray for world peace.
Help us to realize that peace begins at home.
May we solve family problems through thoughtful consideration of nonviolent alternatives.
Help us to realize that we can be models of peacemakers.
May we teach our classes a process for nonviolent problem solving.
Help us to realize that we are responsible for making our peaceful views known.
May we share our concerns for world peace with those responsible in our government.

Dear God . . .
The world you created for us is in danger. Nations have stockpiled nuclear weapons that may be used to destroy our earth.

Please give us the strength and courage to work for peace. Help us to make peace a priority in our daily lives.
Help us to realize the importance of our quest. The time is short. Guide us in our work for peace.
Amen.

The Process of Resolving Conflict

I assess the behavior of each new class to see how soon my "Prison Speech" is required. The requirement varies with each class. This is how my speech came to be.

One day, while I was playing the guitar at a worship service in one of the Oregon prisons, I became acquainted with one of the inmates. After the service, he told me that he was serving a life sentence for murder. Had this gifted young musician killed someone? Impossible, I thought, but sadly it was true. In a fit of anger, he took someone's life. He would give everything he owned to change that day. He cannot. When I was leaving, he said, "I've had a bad temper all my life. Just tell your fourth graders that you can solve problems without hitting someone." After the first fight, I tell my class this young man's story.

Unfortunately, one story doesn't ensure a peaceful year. A specific program is necessary to give children alternatives to violent behavior. It's our responsibility as adults to create an environment where violence isn't an option.

Before a program of nonviolent conflict resolution may begin, the students must understand three basic principles:

• We have dignity because others recognize and respect our rights.
• Others have the same right to dignity and recognition of their rights.
• When problems arise, we can find nonviolent solutions.

We follow a five-point plan of action for conflict resolution.

• Each person relates his or her side without interruption.
• The teacher paraphrases each side to clarify: "You said Jeff bumped into you while you were walking down the hall?" Student answers. "And you said Troy shoved you first?" The student responds.
• The students and teacher decide together on a solution.
• All involved evaluate their behavior so everyone can learn from the mistakes. "What can we do so this problem won't occur again?"
• The students and teacher exchange a sign of reconciliation.

While this seems like a long process, it isn't. Students should be actively engaged in the resolution process rather than waste time in the "he-bumped-me," "no-I-didn't" routine.

Once the students are comfortable with this process, they will solve minor problems with the five-point plan themselves. Then they can report to the teacher how they resolved the conflict.

Let's review the process another way . . .

Step One:	"What happened?" State problem. Each person gets uninterrupted time.
Step Two:	"Is this what you said?" Teacher restates the problem.
Step Three:	"Where do we go from here?" Students and teacher decide on a course of action. It may be a simple apology, a trip to the Consequence Box, or a conference with parents.
Step Four:	"Have we been here before?" What can be done next time so we won't be again? What signs will we watch for so our behavior doesn't become a problem?
Step Five:	"Is Peace Possible?" Students and facilitator exchange sign of reconciliation.

(Please see Activity 25.)

Conflict Resolution in the Classroom

Keep the following tips in mind when problem-solving in the classroom or at home.

1. Have a special place where problems are discussed and solved. When students have a problem, they can go to that special area to discuss it. "Please go back to the rug and talk it over," can be heard in many classrooms.

2. When the students have two stories and can't agree on what happened, resolution will be difficult. Therefore, the students are given a specific time, usually five minutes, to agree on one story. Then the conflict can be resolved.

3. If the conflict is over an object, a ball, pencil, or toy, it goes in a box. When the conflict is resolved, the object is returned to its rightful owner.

4. If many students are involved in the conflict—possibly over a game, if no one was hurt and they all just want to argue, and your headache will get worse if you hear one more word—have everyone write down their version of the story. This approach has several advantages: you get a few moments of peace and quiet, the children get an opportunity to have their say, and everyone is happy.

5. Plan for conflict times. Certain times of day or certain seasons bring more tension. Have an activity or review ready then for possible conflict. If a problem does arise, you can help solve it without the rest of the class just sitting there waiting for something to do. The key is to *be prepared*.

It takes time and effort to help students learn to problem-solve and resolve conflicts nonviolently. It also takes patience and practice. However, this activity is worth all our time and effort. Too many people in our world hit first and ask questions later. We must keep our students from joining their ranks.

Learning to Deal With Conflict

A fantasy: You agree with everyone at breakfast because disagreement is unknown to you. You have the same thing to eat because facing the decision to choose anything new is unimaginable. The newspaper reports only unanimous votes and harmonious activities. The classroom is a delightful place with all students learning without anger or frustration. Games are peaceful because there are no winners or losers, competition isn't known. The evening TV reports another day of trust and cooperation among all people.

Unrealistic? Of course it is. Conflict surrounds us each day and is a part of our lives. Children may not be aware of the latest international conflict, but every child, in his or her own world of family, friends, and school, experiences an overwhelming amount of conflict each day. When the majority of people in a society fear they may become the victims of violent crime, when one out of three marriages ends in divorce, when more than one adult in ten uses drugs as a way of escaping conflict, the issue of war and peace must be seen as a matter of personal as well as global survival.

For all of that, we rarely ask children to study conflict and to learn how to deal with it. Usually the matter comes up only in the middle of a conflict. Jim hits Joey and we shout, "Break it up. We don't have fighting here." But trying to teach a child about conflict in the middle of a fight is like trying to teach someone about gravity while he is plunging to the ground from a fourth floor window. Children need to study conflict objectively, to see it as a simple fact of life, and to experience ways to control it. (Please see Activity 20.)

Learning About Conflict . . .

1. Most conflicts begin when two wants collide. The idea of a want is very real to children. They will be able to write or describe dozens of things they want. The concept of "wants in collision" is also familiar to them. Have them describe occasions when their desires clashed with someone else's. For example:

• They want to watch T.V. and their parents want them to play outside.
• They want to eat candy now and their parents want them to wait until after dinner.

List how a teacher's wants may clash with those of the students, or vice versa. (See Activity 21.)

2. Make a collection of pictures from magazines and newspapers that represent conflict and non-conflict

situations. In small groups, have the children ask the following about their group of pictures.

• What is happening in the picture?
• Are there two clashing wants?
• How do you think the people are feeling?
• How is the conflict being expressed (words, expressions, weapons)?

In the larger classroom setting, the students can talk about their discoveries. Then have the whole class answer this question: Are all conflicts harmful to someone?

3. Have each student keep a conflict diary for one week. When did wants-in-collision occur? What happened after each collision? What patterns are helpful or harmful? What does our diary tell us about the level of peace in our life? (Please see Activities 22 and 24.)

4. What does it mean to be human? Have students list ten things that they can do that an animal cannot do. Then discuss how we react in each of the given situations. This is also a good activity for role playing.

• Someone calls you a name.
• You touch a hot stove.
• A dog barks at you.
• You get scolded for not doing your homework.
• A family member gets hurt.
• Someone pushes you down the stairs.

5. Anger is a very strong emotion. We often try to get even with those who have wronged us. Before we act, we must think and put out anger in proper perspective. Have students ask themselves:

• What am I feeling?
• Why am I frustrated?
• Do I have a right to be angry?
• What shall I do with my anger?
• Can I satisfy my needs without hurting another person?
• Have I really been wronged?
• What is my next step?

Taking a few minutes to analyze the situation, thinking before acting, means we have put anger in proper perspective.

6. Conflicts occur daily. Have students fill out Activity 22 by finding classmates who have dealt with these conflicts. Then have students discuss what they learned about conflict. (Please see Activity 22.)

7. Collect newspapers/magazine articles about peacemakers (see Activity 26). Create a bulletin board or booklet about people working for peace.

A Questionnaire on Conflict

When you have a problem
with someone do you:

	Usually	Sometimes	Never
Avoid the person?	_____	_____	_____
Try to reach a compromise?	_____	_____	_____
Complain or whine until you get your way?	_____	_____	_____
Fight it out physically?	_____	_____	_____
Get another person to decide who is right?	_____	_____	_____
Change the subject?	_____	_____	_____
Give up?	_____	_____	_____
Try to understand the other person's side?	_____	_____	_____
Admit that you are wrong even though you don't think you are?	_____	_____	_____

Conflict: Wants in Collision

By _____

1. What does the word "conflict" mean? _____

_____

2. Describe a conflict you have experienced in the classroom. _____

_____

3. Describe a conflict you have experienced at home. _____

_____

4. Think of a conflict you experienced in the last week. What are the two clashing "wants"? What were you feeling? How was the conflict resolved?

_____

_____

5. Are all conflicts harmful to someone? Why? _____

_____

Learning About My Conflicts

By _____

Conflicts occur daily. Find a person to sign each box. Then discuss what you learned about conflict.

Have you ever had a conflict about one of the following?

Being first in line	What to watch on TV	Taking care of younger members of the family
Using art supplies	Doing homework	Coming in from play
Cleaning up your bedroom	Sharing toys	Walking or riding to school
Privacy	Last piece of dessert	Being the captain of a team
What time to go to bed	Doing the dishes	Who holds the end of the jump rope

My Conflict Diary

By _____

These are the conflicts I encountered during a school week.

MONDAY
TUESDAY
WEDNESDAY
THURSDAY
FRIDAY

Thinking It Over!
When did wants in collision occur?
What happened after each collision?
What patterns are helpful or harmful?
What does my diary tell me about the level of peace in my life?

Looking at Conflict

By _____

Under each category, list some situations that caused you to:

Blame Others

_____

_____

_____

_____

Use Verbal Abuse

_____

_____

_____

_____

Hit Someone

_____

_____

_____

_____

Think Up Excuses

_____

_____

_____

_____

Nonviolent Conflict Resolution

By _____

Our five point plan of action to resolve a conflict nonviolently is:

1. _____

2. _____

3. _____

4. _____

5. _____

Please illustrate how this plan works in our school.

_____

_____

_____

_____

Why is nonviolent conflict resolution important to you?

_____

_____

_____

_____

Peacemaker: Dr. Martin Luther King, Jr.

By _____

Research Dr. Martin Luther King, Jr. and answer the following questions.

What problems did Dr. Martin Luther King, Jr. see in our society?

_____
_____
_____
_____

What did he decide to do?

_____
_____
_____
_____

What did Dr. King say about nonviolence?

_____
_____
_____
_____

How was Dr. Martin Luther King, Jr. a peacemaker?

_____
_____
_____
_____

What lesson did you learn from this man's life?

_____
_____
_____
_____

Peace

By _____

1. What does the word *peace* mean? _____

2. Jesus said, "Blessed are the peacemakers." What did he mean? _____
_____
_____

3. Name three peacemakers. _____
_____
_____

4. Write about a time when you were a peacemaker. _____
_____
_____
_____

5. Do you think the United States is a peacemaker? Why? _____
_____
_____

My Opinion Is Important

By _____

	Agree?	Disagree?
1. It is better for the United States to sell arms to the world than for someone else to do it.		
2. Wherever there are weapons, they will eventually be used.		
3. I believe selling arms can promote peace.		
4. The sale of arms is a political decision and should not be considered from a moral viewpoint.		
5. The United States is morally responsible for any killing done by a United States made weapon.		
6. It is immoral for a Christian, following Jesus' example, to own any kind of weapon.		
7. I believe the United States should greatly reduce the sale of arms to other countries.		
8. I would support a proposal to create arms-free regions of the world.		
9. I believe that world peace is possible.		

CHAPTER FOUR

Teaching in the Nuclear Age

Children of today worry about nuclear war and destruction of the Earth. They feel isolated and need a variety of ways to feel more empowered and hopeful. They need a safe place to express their fears and be reassured that adults are trying to solve the problems facing our Earth.

Working in a Primary Classroom

The first task of the primary teacher is to *listen.* Children need to talk about their fears of the dark, being lost, having their parents get divorced or die, or experiencing an earthquake, tornado, or volcanic eruption. In other words, begin discussions and activities about fears that already exist.

A primary classroom is not an appropriate setting to debate the nuclear question. Children of this age need to discuss fears, and learn and practice nonviolent conflict-resolution process. Games of cooperation need to be emphasized during breaks and classroom activity periods.

Suggestions for Primary Classroom

Make a "Fears Book." Invite the children to draw pictures of all the things or events they fear. While drawing the pictures is important, the discussions that follow are vital. Leave the "Fears Books" out for the children to look at during spare time. It is often reassuring to know that others have the same fears.
Design a class peace symbol.
Design a peace poster with a simple message.
Draw pictures of a peaceful future.
Write five rules for a peaceful world. Share your rules with other classes.
Learn the word "peace" in other languages.

• Read together four poems from *Where the Sidewalk Ends,* by Shel Silverstein (Harper & Row, 1974), and have discussions relating to each poem.

"Where the Sidewalk Ends" (page 64)
Discuss peaceful places or special places where we feel safe. Students may also draw pictures about their favorite peaceful places.
"Hug-O-War" (page 9)
Read aloud and then discuss winning and losing. Discuss changing the rules for old games so they become games of cooperation instead of games of competition.
"Helping" (page 101)
Discuss ways students work together in the classroom and at home.
"I Won't Hatch" (page 127)
The students love to act out this poem about a chick who refuses to hatch because of all the terrible things going on in the world. Discuss the poem and then write a list about all the good things the chick might find if he breaks out of the egg shell.

• Read the following resource books, which have hundreds of games of cooperation. Everyone plays, everyone has fun, and everyone wins. Buy them or borrow them from your local library and share the fun of cooperation with your students.

Everybody's A Winner: A Kid's Guide to New Sports and Fitness, by Tom Schneider (Little, Brown and Company, 1976).

A Manual On Nonviolence and Children. An excellent book for parents and primary teachers. May be purchased from: Nonviolence and Children Program, Friends Peace Committee, 1515 Cherry Street, Philadelphia, Penn. 19102. ($5.00 plus 50¢ postage)
More New Games: and Playful Ideas from the New Games Foundation. (Doubleday) Found in local bookstores.
The New Games Book: Play Hard, Play Fair, Nobody Hurt. Edited by Andrew Fluegelman (Doubleday). Found in local bookstores and libraries.

• It is often the custom to have an End-of-the-Year Picnic complete with races and contests. Why not complement your closing activity with games of cooperation rather than competition? Then everyone goes home a "winner."
• Students need time during the class period to take a deep breath and calm their individual energies. Allow time for reflection and centering activities. If you are interested in helping change inner disquiet into more productive and creative energy, the following resource book will interest you.

A Peaceable Classroom: Activities to Calm and Free Student Energies, by Merrill Harmin and Saville Sax (Winston Press).

Working in an Intermediate Classroom

Children from nine to twelve are collectors of facts, and nuclear facts are often frightening. We need to inform children, not scare them, and lower tension levels. Children in tbe intermediate grades need adult support and protection. They need to see that adults care about their future and actively work for a peaceful world.

Activities for an Intermediate Classroom

Review the conflict activities in Chapter Three. Students should be able to define conflict, identify conflicts that occur daily and evaluate their own responses when conflict situations occur.
2. Collect current newspaper/magazine articles about world conflicts. Put articles on a bulletin board or make a class booklet.
3. Create a time line that describes key events in the arms race.
4. Create a world map showing countries that have nuclear capabilities and those that do not.
5. Have the students draw a picture to illustrate "A Peaceful Place to Live" (see ????).
6. Design a world peace flag. What colors are significant? What do the symbols mean?

7. Using blank address labels, have students design a peace message that can be used on the back of envelopes.
8. Use classroom windows to share a peace message with the world.
9. Study what organizations in your area are working on peace issues. Ask if they can provide a guest speaker or film for your classroom.
10. Learn peace songs and then share them with the school community. Some suggestions: "Last Night I Had the Strangest Dream" by Ed McCurdy, 1950; "Let There Be Peace on Earth" by Jill Jackson and Sy Miller, 1955; "Vine and Fig Tree" (Traditional); "I'm Gonna Study War No More" (Traditional).
11. Organize a Children's Peace March.
12. Encourage children to participate in games of cooperation instead of competition. (Please see /8 in the Primary section for suggestions on resources available.)
13. Intermediate-grade students are good letter writers. Have them write to the President or members of Congress to express their views about the arms race or other areas of concern.

President _____
The White House
Washington, D.C. 20500

or telephone and leave
a message . . .
(202) 456-1414

Address Senators:
The Honorable _____
U.S. Senate
Washington, D.C. 20510

Dear Senator _____:

Address Representatives:
The Honorable _____
U.S. House of Representatives
Washington, D.C. 20515

Dear (Mr., Mrs., Miss., Ms.) _____:

Remind students to:

• Write in their own words because form letters do not receive the same attention.
• Address one issue only and clearly state their point.
• Ask questions about bills or issues of concern.
• Write more than once and let their elected officials know that they are committed to action.

14. It has been said that George Washington was "first in war and first in peace." What does this saying mean? Who would be "first in peace" in our classroom, our neighborhood, our city, our country, our world?

15. Abraham Lincoln wanted justice for all and his Emancipation Proclamation changed the course of history in this country. Ask the students who works for justice today in your city? your state? your country? What causes do they work to help further?

16. Use a dictionary, magazines and newspapers to look up any words or concepts you want to know about. Create a vocabulary list of words connected with the arms race.

17. Write and illustrate acrostic poems.

P is for	H is for
E is for	O is for
A is for	P is for
C is for	E is for
E is for	

18. Write a story about what you would like your life to be like in twenty years. What will the newspaper headlines read in twenty years?

19. Have students correspond with the students in another school in another country. This is an opportunity to sponsor a Soviet-American exchange. For further information, write:

International Friendship League
22 Batterymarch Street
Boston, Mass. 02109
(617) 523-4273

Working in a Junior High Classroom

Junior high students are ready to examine and study nuclear issues. Several activities are listed here, but junior high teachers need to explore the many resources available for older students. Please see the list of resources at the end of this section.

Activities for a Junior High Classroom

1. Have the students develop a nuclear vocabulary. Key words might include:

B-52	MAD
bi-lateral	megaton
counterforce	MIRV
Cruise missile	MX Missiles
deploy	NATO
deterence	neutron bomb
first strike	SALT
capability	START
freeze	tactical weapons
ground zero	TRIAD
Hiroshima & Nagasaki	Trident
ICBM	unilateral
	warhead

2. Have the students answer a questionnaire on the nuclear world. Sample questions might include:
What comes to mind when you hear the word "nuclear"?
What ideas come to mind when you hear the word "peace"?
Do you think a nuclear war will occur in your lifetime? Who is responsible for the arms race?
Do you think the threat of nuclear war is increasing? Why?
Do you think you could survive a nuclear attack? Your city? Your state? Your country? Your Earth?
Have nuclear issues affected your plans for the future? How?
What would you like United States policy on nuclear weapons to include?
What involvement have you had with the nuclear issue? What is your hope for the future?

3. Write a letter to your city newspaper expressing your opinions on the nuclear issue. (Please see #14 in the Intermediate section for further ideas on letter writing.)

4. Take a poll of your school or neighborhood community on feelings and thoughts about nuclear weapons. Share your findings with class members.

5. Form a Peace Club and share ideas and feelings. Work together to distribute information to others.

6. Study civil defense plans for your area. Evaluate current plans.

7. Study and discuss questions such as:
What is the difference between arms control and disarmament?
What are the goals of current United States nuclear activity?
What was SALT I and what did it accomplish? How about SALT II?
What is fear of the Soviet Union based on?
What would the world be like after a nuclear war?
Who gains from the nuclear arms build-up? Who loses?
Is military spending good for the economy?
What are the major obstacles to world peace?
Are nuclear weapons meant to be used? If you were President, would you use them?
What do you think is the best way to avoid nuclear war?

8. Have the students research Nobel Peace Prize winners and then give a report to the class.

9. Have the students nominate individuals for this year's Nobel Peace Prize. Students must have reasons for their nominations. Have the class vote on a Peacemaker for the year.

10. Call the Nuclear Arms Control Hotline: (202) 543-0006. This hotline is available twenty-four hours a day offering a three-minute taped message on arms control and military budget legislation, and upcoming key votes in Congress. The hotline is sponsored by the Council for a Livable World. Let your representatives know how you stand on legislation referred to in the taped message.

Good Books About Conflict, Peace, and Cooperation

PRIMARY GRADES

The Big Pile of Dirt, by Eleanor Clymer (Holt, Rinehart, & Winston). A pile of dirt is the only good place that the poor children have to play. Some rich people who are trying to beautify the city want the dirt removed but the children find a way to keep their pile of dirt.

The Big War, by Betty Baker (Harper & Row). An I Can Read history book about the rivalry between two groups, each of whom thinks an island belongs to them.

Changes, Changes, by Pat Hutchins (Collier). In this book without words a wooden toy couple build their own house and then they work together creatively to rebuild it elsewhere when it burns down. Stimulates discussion on how we deal with frustrations.

Drummer Hoff, by Barbara Emberly (Prentice-Hall). A simple attractive verse with colorful pictures about building a cannon.

Duck in the Gun, by Joy Cawley (Doubleday & Co.). Continuing commitment to life rather than death is central to this story of a war prevented when a duck nests in a cannon.

The Hating Book, by Charlotte Zolotow (Harper & Row). An excellent story about friendships and childhood disagreements, classroom communication patterns, and the importance of making ourselves clear. The game of Telephone may follow the discussion of this story: a message is started at one end of the room, whispered from one person to another, and then shared aloud by the last person.

Let's Be Enemies, by Janice May Udry, illustrated by Maurice Sendak (Scholastic Books). This delightful story is about two little boys involved in a power struggle.

Naja, the Snake, and Mangus, the Mongoose, by Oliver Kirkpatrick (Doubleday). A Jamaican parable about rethinking roles and the peaceful solution discovered by habitual enemies. A snake and a mongoose learn to take pleasure in each other's cleverness and company.

No Fighting, No Biting, by Else Minarik, illustrated by Maurice Sendak (Harper and Row). A delightful story with a powerful message.

Potatoes, Potatoes, by Anita Lobel (Bowman/Noble). A story about a mother's efforts to shield her two sons from war, their eventual involvement, and the final resolution of the war.

The Quarreling Book, by Charlotte Zolotow (Harper & Row). A bad mood is passed from adults to the children and frustration builds. The negative spiral becomes positive and friendliness returns to the scene. A good discussion starter on how we can bring peace into our circle of family and friends.

The Story of Ferdinand, by Monro Leaf (Viking Press). The classic story of the bull who didn't want to fight.

The Stranger, by Kjell Ringi (Random House, Inc.). A fable about people who bring out their cannon against a giant stranger. When they finally get to know him, the stranger is invited to stay in their country. This story requires us to examine our fears realistically.

Surviving Fights With Your Brothers and Sisters, by Joy Wilt (Word, Incorporated). This excellent volume of the Ready-Set-Grow series discusses why brothers and sisters fight, what happens when they fight, and how to handle the fights when they occur.

The Tears of the Dragon, by Hirusuki Hamanda. One boy does not believe the village rumor that the dragon who lives on the mountain is evil. He invites the dragon to his birthday party. This book clearly points out the role of misinformation and prejudice in creating walls.

The Terrible Thing That Happened At Our House, by Marge Blaine (Parents Magazine Press). Mom goes back to work and then everything starts to change. One of the children runs away and the family has a meeting to work out solutions to everyone's difficulties.

INTERMEDIATE

Candles in the Dark, by Brinton, McShuter, and Schroeder (Hemlock Press). Fifty-one stories on peacemaking situations.

Earth: Our Crowded Spaceship, by Isaac Asimov (John Day). An excellent account of the many problems facing "spaceship Earth," written for middle graders.

The Game on Thatcher Island, by T. Degens (Viking). Harry is flattered when a group of older boys invite him to participate in their game of war on Thatcher Island. His elation disappears when the game takes a terrifying turn.

How Children Stopped the Wars, by Jan Wahl (Farrar, Straus, and Giroux). The story of a shepherd boy who sets out to stop wars and persuades hundreds of children to follow his leadership.

Let's Cry for Peace, by Hiroshima A- Bombed Teachers Association. This 50¢ booklet is available from: Peace

Resource Center, Box 1183, Wilmington College, Wilmington, Ohio 45177. Personal stories of two children, plus moving poems and songs for peace.

My Shalom, My Peace, by Jacob Zim (McGraw-Hill). A moving collection of paintings and poems on the theme of peace by Arab and Jewish children.

A Peaceable Kingdom: The Shaker Abecedarius, illustrated by Alice Provensen and Martin Provensen (Viking). An alphabet verse with clear, quietly detailed illustrations supplemented on nearly every page by inscriptions representing Shaker thought.

Peace Is You and Me, by Florence Weiner (Avon). A collection of children's writings about peace.

Sadako and the Thousand Paper Cranes, by Eleanor Coerr (Dell Yearling Book). A fictionalized account based on a true story about an eleven-year-old Japanese girl who is found to have leukemia resulting from radiation exposure.

The Tomato Patch, by William Wondriska (Holt). Two warlike kingdoms become peaceful by means of a young girl's tomato patch.

The War Party, by William O. Steele (Harcourt, Brace, Jovanovich). A Let Me Read book about a young Native American who looks forward to his first battle. However, when he participates in an attack on a neighboring village, he is horrified by the violence that surrounds him.

JUNIOR HIGH

Alan and Naomi, by Myron Levoy (Harper & Row). A powerful portrait of Naomi, who has been traumatized by having witnessed Nazi brutality to her father in France during the war.

Conrad's War, by Andrew Davies (Crown). A strange story about a boy's fantasies about war, killing, and guns.

In Search of Peace: Winners of the Nobel Peace Prize, 1901-1975, (Abingdon). Information about the Nobel Peace Prize and its recipients emphasizing efforts by individuals to keep humanity at peace.

Journey Home, by Yoshiko Uchida (Atheneum). A Japanese-American girl and her family attempt to reconstruct their lives after their release from an American concentration camp.

Nisei Daughter, by Monica Itoi Sone (University of Washington Press). A unique and moving personal account of a Japanese-American family's relocation during World War II.

Transport 7-41-R, by T. Degens (Viking). A young girl travels from the Russian sector of defeated Germany to Cologne on a transport carrying returning refugees in 1946. On one level, this is an adventure story. On another level it is a powerful statement on the devastation of war.

The Watch on Patterick Fell, by Fay Sampson (Greenwillow Books). Set in England some years in the future, the story postulates a situation where wide-spread protests force the shut-down of nuclear power plants. This book holds interest and poses good questions about nuclear power.

Resources

IMPORTANT BOOKS FOR EDUCATORS:

Black Rain, by Masuji Ibuse (Kodansha International). A novel about a family who lived through Hiroshima in 1945.

The Fate of the Earth, by Jonathan Schell (Alfred Knopf). An essay on nuclear weapons and their implications for the future of the planet.

National Defense, by James Fallows (Random House). Outlines the priorities the author believes must be established to develop a reliable and affordable defense system.

Nuclear Madness, What You Can Do, by Dr. Helen Caldicott (Autumn Press). A simple and powerful introduction to the topic by a passionate opponent of nuclear power and weapons.

Nuclear War: What's In It for You?, by Ground Zero Campaign (Pocket Books). An educational resource for those interested in developing an informed perspective on the threat of nuclear war.

Peacemaking, by Barbara Stanford (Bantam Books). This excellent paperback is subtitled "a guide to conflict resolution for individuals, groups, and nations."

Primer on the Arms Race, by Educators for Social Responsibility, 639 Massachusetts Avenue, Cambridge, Mass. 02139. A collection of articles giving background information on the arms race, including a section on starting a local chapter of Educators for Social Responsibility.

Restoring American Power in a Dangerous Decade, by Richard Barnet (Simon and Schuster). An outstanding discussion of the philosophy and use of nuclear weapons as part of our foreign policy.

War and Peace in Literature, by Lucy Dougal (World Without War Publications, 67 E. Madison, Suite 1417,

Chicago, Ill. 60603). An annotated listing of 354 literary works from the western tradition that hold a mirror up to war. ($5.00 plus 75c postage)

CURRICULUM MATERIALS FOR EDUCATORS:

U.S.-U.S.S.R. Reconciliation Program
The Fellowship of Reconciliation
P.O. Box 271
Nyack, N.Y. 10960
(914) 358-4601

Send for information on:
U.S.-U.S.S.R. Photo Exchange
Seeds of Hope
An Art Project
Project for Writers

Items to Order:
Buttons that say "peace" in English and Russian.
1-50 50¢ each, over 100 25¢ each.
Peace Studies Curriculum

Building Blocks to Peace	K
Peace Is in Our Hands	1-6
Learning Peace	7-12

Order from: Jane Addams Peace Assoc.
Philadelphia, Penn. 10107
Seed packet envelopes with note paper to send to Soviet and American Representatives, bearing a message of friendship in Russian and English. Two free, packet of ten, $1.00
Soviet Reading Packet, $3.00
Order from: SANE
711 G Street, S.E.
Washington, D.C. 20003
(202) 546-7100
U.S.-U.S.S.R. Reconciliation Directory. Includes booklist. $1.00 Please add 20¢ for shipping.
Educating for Peace and Justice: A Manual for Teachers

I. National Dimensions	$9.00
II. Global Dimensions	$9.00
III. Religious Dimensions	$9.00
IV. Teacher Background Readings	$5.00

(Prices include postage)
Available from: The Institute for Peace and Justice
2747 Rutger
St. Louis, Mo. 63104

Evaluating Textbooks

We all need to evaluate the books we use in class to see how they deal with the question of peace.

Peace
1. When does the text use the term peace?
2. Does the text distinguish kinds of peace?
3. Does the text refer to war? Does it describe war as inevitable? as justified in some instances? as morally wrong? as a problem?
4. Are the causes of war mentioned? Are several causes of war given? Are these greatly simplified? Why does the book deal with the subject of war?
5. Are ways suggested in which one can work to end war?

Conflict
1. Is conflict normal for people? Is it wrong? Am I a better person if I do not get involved in conflicts?
2. How do people deal with conflicts? What are the alternatives to violence in resolving conflict?
3. Does the book teach that forgivensss is the only way of resolving conflict? Is "turning the other cheek" the only answer suggested?
4. Does the text teach that law is a valid way of resolving conflict? Is cooperation the best response to the problem of conflict?

World Community
1. How does the text deal with differences in cultures, races, and peoples?
2. How does it treat prejudice?
3. Is there any reference to an examination of the common qualities, needs, and hopes of human beings? the similarities among all peoples?
4. Does the text inculcate a sense of belonging and a sense of responsibility not only to the local community and the national community, but also to the world community?

Nonviolence
1. Is nonviolence mentioned? defined?
2. Does nonviolence, as it is defined in the text, include a commitment to social change? Who are the heroes?
3. Is nonviolence presented as unreal? as nice, but . . . ?
4. Are examples of nonviolent action given? Are these examples ones which involve more than individual heroism, good will, and generosity? Are political solutions considered?

CHAPTER FIVE

One Earth, One Family

Humans have the same basic needs. They share the Earth as their home. Chapter Five explores the many ways the people of the Earth are interdependent. As all people are members of the "People of God," they all must be respected and appreciated.

Dear God . . .
Help us to see the beauty of your creations, the wide variety of individual appearances and personalities.

Help us to take a new look at each person to see the unique gifts and talents they have to offer.

Help us to recognize the unique contributions of each person. Help us to look beyond appearances, handicaps, or racial characteristics.

Jesus, the teacher, never excluded anyone from his message of love. Help us to accept all people.

Jesus, the leader, chose his Apostles from all occupations and told his disciples to go forth and teach all nations. Help us to be aware and appreciate the cultural gifts of others.

Jesus, the worker of miracles, recognized the special needs of the blind, the lame, and the sick. Help us to look beyond the white cane or wheelchair to see that special person with gifts to contribute.

Jesus, the Prince of Peace, asked all peoples to live and work together. Help us to strive for non-violent resolution of conflicts in our homes, neighborhoods, cities, and countries.

Dear God . . . Help us to follow your son's example. Give us the confidence to be free to love ourselves and love others. Help us to be free to recognize and appreciate the gifts of others.

Dear God . . . The signs of harvest are all around us, the promise of spring fulfilled. Help us to nurture the talents of our staff members and the children in our classrooms. May they continue to grow in an environment of encouragement and support. May we learn to see each person as one of God's special creations, and through the harvest of their talents build a world community of peace. Amen.

The Time Is Now

WAR ESCALATES IN THE MIDDLE EAST
FAMINE FACES MANY AFRICAN COUNTRIES
ONE OUT OF FOUR SENIOR CITIZENS IS HUNGRY
"I'm too busy."
"I'm too tired."
"I have enough to worry about already."

50% UNEMPLOYMENT FACES OUR NATIVE AMERICANS
POPE JOHN PAUL II CALLS FOR REDISTRIBUTION
OF WORLD RESOURCES
RACIAL TENSIONS EXPLODE AT HIGH SCHOOL
"Not another meeting!"
"I'm not good at speaking out."
"There's never enough time."

NUCLEAR WEAPONS SOLD TO THIRD WORLD NATIONS
ANOTHER CHILD MISSING IN ATLANTA
EDUCATIONAL SCORES DECLINE AGAIN
"What good is one person?"
"But I'll miss my TV show."
"All you hear about is the negative."

U.S. HAS 6% OF THE WORLD'S POPULATION
U.S. USES 50% OF THE WORLD'S RESOURCES
U.S. USES 33% OF THE WORLD'S ENERGY

One Earth . . .

Children are children are children. No matter where we look—Chile, China, or Canada—many common threads run through childhood years. Children everywhere enjoy hide and seek, jump rope, ice cream, candles, and birthday cakes. In fact, children around the world have shared many common experiences. Like children, we are more alike than we are different. We have all shared happy moments, cried over a sad event or a bad day, felt disappointment, anger, excitement, anxiety, and joy. We have all been tired and felt hungry. Thus, in many ways we are similar. We are members of a world community.

As we begin each class, let's remember our special relationship with the world community. A fourth-grade class wrote this World Prayer. You may either write one with your own class as an October project or use this as a sample:

> Today we remember the people of the world, the children in schools, the parents at work, the lonely, the sick, and the homeless. May each person have a happy moment today, a special time with a friend, a quiet time to think and a time to play. May God bless all my brothers and sisters today.

With your World Prayer, you might have the children select one place in the world to mention especially. Children love to pick out special places on the globe or on maps. This also will help in geography awareness skills.

Nation to Nation Participation Map . . .

This activity would certainly vary with the age of your students. The little ones can do it as a group, and older students can do it individually or in teams.

Using a different color for each category, indicate on the world map your connections with people in other countries. Categories can include:

• Routes you have traveled.
• Countries where you have lived or visited.
• Locations of relatives.
• Countries having the same religion.
• Countries you own things from.

(Please see Activity 29.)

Since we belong to a world community, it is helpful if children can place themselves in time and space. Ask each child to complete and recite this sentence. My name is _____. I live at _____, in the city of _____ in the state of _____, in the country _____ on the continent of _____ in the Western Hemisphere on the planet Earth.

(Please see Activity 32.)

Students at Holy Redeemer School, in Portland, Oregon, made up the following song. Your class may create their own tune to fit the words.

Chorus: I'm a special person in a special place,
Special person in a special place,
Special person in a special place,
There's a season for all things.
Verse 1: I live in a neighborhood, (3)
I'm a special person in a special place.
Verse 2: My neighborhood is in the city of *(Portland)*, (3)
I'm a special person in a special place.
Verse 3: *(Portland)* is in the state of *(Oregon)*, (3)
I'm a special person in a special place.
Verse 4: *(Oregon)* is in the U.S.A., (3)
I'm a special person in a special place.
Verse 5: The U.S.A. is on the planet Earth, (3)
I'm a special person in a special place.
Verse 6: The Earth is part of the universe, (3)
I'm a special person in a special place.

The Shakertown Pledge

Recognizing that the earth and the fulness thereof is a gift from our gracious God, and that we are called to cherish, nurture, and provide loving stewardship for the earth's resources; and

Recognizing that life itself is a gift and a call to responsibility, joy, and celebration,

I make the following declarations:
1. I declare myself to be a world citizen.
2. I commit myself to lead an ecologically sound life.
3. I commit myself to lead a life of creative simplicity and to share my personal wealth with the world's poor.
4. I commit myself to join others in reshaping institutions to bring about a more just global society in which each person has full access to the needed resources for their physical, emotional, intellectual, and spiritual growth.
5. I commit myself to occupational accountability, and in so doing I will seek to avoid the creation of products which cause harm to others.
6. I affirm the gift of my body, and commit myself to its proper nourishment and physical well-being.
7. I commit myself to examine continually my relations with others, and to attempt to relate honestly, morally, and lovingly to those around me.
8. I commit myself to personal renewal through prayer, meditation, and study.
9. I commit myself to responsible participation in a community of faith.

You can take this pledge and do yourself a favor. You can also do the world a favor by sending your name and address to: Shakertown Pledge Group, 4719 Cedar Street, Philadelphia, Penn. 19143.

Sound Familiar?

"Children, here is your new play area. Girls, there is the house; boys, there is the workshop."

"The Vietnamese are very skilled in the math area."

"Boys, please help me move the piano. Girls, will you please water the plants."

"Mrs. Smith, will you clean up the kitchen. And Mr. Johnson, will you be in charge of the Student Government?

"Mainstreaming handicapped children is unfair to the classroom teacher. Who wants a wheelchair in the classroom?"

"Boys are better in math and science; girls are better in reading and in writing."

"Black children excel in sports."

"Mrs. Simpson is really too old to try any of the new teaching techniques."

"Girls, you can play jump rope. Boys, you will play basketball today."

"Boys, why can't you be nice and quiet like the girls?"

"Blind people really are missing out from the important things in life."

Each of us has said or experienced one of the above statements at one time or another. An occasional statement in this vein is bad enough. However, if our thinking puts individuals in categories because of their gender or race, we are in trouble because we are creating unjust expectations of the people with whom we meet and work. We have failed to recognize the inherent dignity of each individual. We are putting limits on people which don't allow or encourage them to develop to their greatest potential.

Look Around, Think About It

- Are the pictures in our classrooms multicultural?
- Are the following racial groups represented: White? Black? Native American? Hispanic? Asian?
- Do the pictures show racial stereotypes?
- Are there pictures of women as doctors, judges, business executives, truck drivers, or forest rangers?
- Are there pictures of men as nurses, librarians, childcare workers, or dancers?
- (Please see Activities 29, 30, 33, 34.)

Many of the curriculum materials we use today are sexist. While it is impossible to discard all materials that fall into this category, we not only must be aware of the situation but must also discuss it in the classroom when appropriate.

- Do our texts usually characterize boys as active, involved in sports, independent, using initiative, earning money, solving problems, and receiving recognition?

- Are girls characterized as quiet, fragile, passive, fearful, receiving help?
- Are boys ever shown showing emotions, being gentle, or holding a baby?
- Are mothers shown engaged in activities other than housework or child-rearing?
- Are fathers shown in roles other than going to work or cutting the lawn?
- Are there any stories about one-parent families or families without children?

Our Need to Be Independent

Materials: one small cup of water, spoon, and napkin for each person.

Directions:
Divide your class into Group A and Group B. Say to them, "Today we will do some role-playing. Now listen carefully: Group A, you are blind, please shut your eyes tightly and sit there quietly. Group B, please go over to the table and get a cup of water, a spoon, and a napkin. When you return to your partner, please introduce yourself and feed him/her the 'vegetable soup' since he/she is very hungry."

(B's then proceed to feed the A's the soup. After five minutes or so have elapsed, the partners switch places and the formerly blind person will go to the table and get the water, spoon, and napkin. Continue as before.)

Read the following two scenes to the children after their role playing.
Scene One: "Hello, my name is Susan and I came to feed you some vegetable soup. Are you very hungry? Good. Now the soup is pretty hot and I hope I don't spill any on you. O.K., here we go. When I say 'Open' just open your mouth wide because the soup is on its way. Oh, very good. Now for another bite. Is it good? Oh dear, I'm sorry I spilled it on you. Let's try again."
Scene Two: "Hello, my name is Martha. How are you today? Are you hungry? Would you like some vegetable soup? Here is the cup. (Guides person's hand to the cup). Here is the spoon. That soup looks good . . . I'm going to get some, too, so we can eat together."
Now discuss the following questions:

- How did you feel being blind?
- How did you feel helping someone?
- Did you feel frustrated? Why? When?
- Did you feel embarrassed? Why? When?

I've used this role-playing experiment with many kinds of groups. Usually 95% of the participants will act out some variety of Scene One. Those few acting out Scene Two have already learned the lesson that all people need a sense of independence and must be allowed to do the activities they are capable of doing.

Role-play the situation again with the attitude of "doing with" rather than "doing for." Isn't there a world of difference?

This lesson needs to be remembered not only when working with handicapped people, but when we work with any human being. We all suffer disabilities of one sort or another. Having others, "do for" us doesn't help the problem; having someone "do with" us might give us the confidence to do it on our own the next time.

(Please see Activity 35.)

Good Books About the Human Family

PRESCHOOL AND PRIMARY GRADES

Amigo, by Byrd Baylor Schweitzer (Macmillan). A little Mexican boy and a prairie dog find and love each other.

Blind Men and the Elephant, by Lillian Quigley (Scribner). In India, six blind men learn how to find the whole truth.

Corduroy, by Don Freeman (Viking). A stuffed bear finds a loving home with a little Black girl.

A Crocodile's Tale, by Jose and Ariane Aruego (Scholastic). It takes a clever monkey to rescue Juan from a smooth-talking crocodile, and to teach an important lesson on gratitude.

Crow Boy, by Taro Yashima (Penguin). A shy Japanese boy is recognized and accepted by his classmates through his teacher's understanding and sympathy.

Did You Carry the Flag Today, Charley?, by Rebecca Caudill (Holt, Rinehart, and Winston). When Charley begins school, his family explains to him that the highest honor is being chosen to "carry the flag," an award each day to the child who is most helpful. In his own unique way, Charley does get to carry the flag, and what he learns on that special day can help us all.

Frog and Toad Are Friends, by Arnold Lobel (Harper and Row). Frog and Toad's adventures are filled with the give and take of friendship.

Grownups Cry Too, by Nancy Hazen (Lollipop Power). Descriptions of different situations in which people cry.

In My Mother's House, by Ann Clark (Viking). The Pueblo Indians engage in daily sharing through community life.

The Quarreling Book, by Charlotte Zolotow (Harper and Row). One person's bad mood makes the next person angry. Soon the entire family is making nasty comments until someone breaks the spiral.

Red Man, White Man, African Chief, by Marguerite Lerner (Lerner Publications). This Brotherhood Award winner explains skin pigmentation to children in simple language and in relation to objects familiar to any child.

INTERMEDIATE GRADES

All of a Kind Family, by Sydney Taylor (Dell). Five little daughters of a Jewish junk dealer on New York's East Side in the early 1900's manage to have a lively time with little money.

Call It Courage, by Armstrong Sperry (Macmillan). A Polynesian boy is determined to conquer his cowardice or die.

Eddie No Name, by Thomas Fall (Scholastic). Eddie wants a name of his own, but when the Whalens take him home from the orphanage for a trial period, everything he does seems to go wrong.

I Feel the Same Way, by Lilian Moore (Atheneum). These poems say that deep down are secret feelngs we all share.

Meaning Well, by Sheila Cole (Watts). A sensitive look at the effects of peer pressure: Lisa is torn between what she knows is right and acceptance by her friends.

Member of the Gang, by Barbara Rinkoff (Scholastic). Bored and tired of being criticized by parents, Woodie joins a street gang. He soon realizes his goals and his family's differ greatly from those of the other Scorpions.

The Pepper Salt Land, by Marilyn Harris (Scholastic). Two 12-year-olds, one Black and one Anglo-American, are confronted with the ugliness of racism in a small Southern community.

Salt Boy, by Mary Perrine (Houghton Mifflin). When a sudden storm threatens the sheep he tends, a Navajo boy makes a wise decision and thereby earns the respect of his father.

Second-Hand Family, by Richard Parker (Bobbs-Merrill). Twelve-year-old Giles is adopted by a family in an English mining town.

UPPER GRADES

About the 'Bnai Bagels, by E. L. Konigsburg (Atheneum). The summer Mark's mother became manager of his Little League team and his best friend moved away seemed to bring more problems than any boy ought to have to endure.

The Boy Who Could Make Himself Disappear, by Kim Platt (Dell). Roger Baxter, new and lonely in New York and with a speech impediment, has a tough time making friends.

Durango Street, by Frank Bonham (Dell). A black boy struggles against gang life in a ghetto; a youth worker seeks to help him.

The Mimosa Tree, by Vera and Bill Cleaver (Harper and Row). A good story about the helplessness of a family in a strange environment losing its sole means of support: the mother.

The Slave Dancer, by Paula Fox (Bradbury Press). The scenes in which Jessie is forced to play his fife to "dance the slaves" for their morning exercises become a haunting tragic experience. A grim but powerful drama.

Very Important Words

By _____

Write a definition for each of these words. Then think of a time you have experienced them.

Prejudice

Sexism

Oppression

Discrimination

Please be ready to share your experiences with your classmates.

Very Important People

By _____

What notable Black person do you admire the most?

    In your own community _____

    In the United States _____

What notable Hispanic person do you admire the most?

    In your own community _____

    In the United States _____

What notable Native American do you admire the most?

    In your own community _____

    In the United States _____

What notable Asian person do you admire the most?

    In your own community _____

    In the United States _____

What notable Anglo-American person do you admire the most?

    In your own community _____

    In the United States _____

What makes a person notable? Why?_____

Nation to Nation Participation

By _____

What countries have you visited? _____

Do you have relatives or friends in other countries? _____

If so, where? _____

What countries are in the news this week? Why? _____

What countries do you own things from? _____

ITEM: _____

_____

_____

COUNTRY: _____

_____

_____

Name three countries you would like to visit. Give a reason for your answer.

_____

_____

_____

A Special Person in a Special Place

By _____

My name is _____.

My street address is _____

in the city of _____,

in the state of _____,

in the country _____,

on the continent of _____,

in the _____Hemisphere _____,

on the planet _____.

I AM A SPECIAL PERSON IN A SPECIAL PLACE.

Native Americans

By _____

1. What does the term "Native American" mean? _____

_____

2. Where did we get the term "Indian"? _____

_____

3. How have Hollywood movies stereotyped Native Americans? _____

_____

4. Do you talk about Indians as though they belong to the past? Why? _____

_____

_____

5. Name three great Native American chiefs who worked for peace. _____

_____

_____

6. What are some of the problems facing Native Americans today? _____

_____

_____

Foreign Friends

By _____

Read the poem below written by Robert Louis Stevenson.

"Foreign Friends"
Little Indian Sioux or Crow,
Little frosty Eskimo
Little Turk or Japanese
Oh! Don't you wish that you were me?

You have seen the scarlet trees,
And the lions overseas;
You have eaten ostrich eggs,
And turned the turtles off their legs.

Such a life is very fine,
But it's not so nice as mine;
You must often as you trod,
Have wearied not to be abroad.

You have curious things to eat,
I am fed on proper meat;
You must dwell beyond the foam,
But I am safe and live at home.

Little Indian Sioux or Crow,
Little frosty Eskimo,
Little Turk or Japanese,
Oh! Don't you wish that you were me?

What words of advice could you give Robert Louis Stevenson about One Earth, One Family?

Reflection: Our Need to Be Independent

By _____

1. What does the word "independent" mean? _____

_____

2. How did you feel being "blind"? _____

_____

3. How did you feel helping someone? _____

_____

4. Were you ever frustrated? Why? When? _____

_____

5. Were you ever embarrassed? Why? When? _____

_____

_____

6. What lesson did this story teach you? _____

_____

7. How do you allow others to feel independent? _____

_____

_____

CHAPTER SIX

Family

The American family has changed. Chapter Six examines two basic influences on the American family—divorce and television. As part of education for peace and justice we must explore their influence on the lives of the children we teach.

Dear God . . .
Help us to love and accept all of your children. May we be sensitive to their special needs and help them to accept their feelings.
Please bless our families.
Help us to share our love for one another.
Help us to share our joys and our sorrows.
Help us to say
"I love you."
"I'm sorry."
"I need you to help me."
Help us to realize that your family comes in many sizes and shapes.
Help us to see that we are all your people.
Help us to see that we are all part of your continuing story of salvation history.
Help us to share our talents and resources with those who need our time and care.

Dear God . . .
Living in the world is not easy. Everywhere we see trauma and pain.
Help us
to live with courage,
to minister to those who need a kind word,
to take the time to realize what a wonderful gift a family can be.
With a growing hope, we face the future knowing that you give your human family many resources.
With a growing conviction, we face the realities of the decade and know our work for peace and justice is not in vain.
With growing love, we see your face in the families of today. We only need to take the time to look. Lord, give us the time and the courage to look. Amen.

The American Family

The American family, one father, one mother, one daughter, and one son. Right? Wrong! Times have changed—the American family has changed. Or maybe it never was like that.

Early American life centered around the family. Fathers worked at home as farmers or tradesmen. Parents nurtured their children, educated them, and taught them a trade. The Industrial Revolution prompted fathers to leave home during daytime hours and children started attending schools.

At the beginning of this century most Americans lived in rural areas. As the industrial age grew, families left small towns and villages to be near centers of work. Families tended to stay together. Grandparents, aunts, uncles, and cousins lived nearby.

Times have changed. To survive economically in the 70's, family members were forced to move often. Many women joined the work force. Few families have relatives near them. Grandparents and other family members are no longer around to provide role models for the children or support for the parents.

What can be done? There are no easy answers. As educators we need to keep three concepts in mind:

- We cannot return to the past. We no longer live in an agriculturally centered society. Times have changed, families have changed. We must work and live with the reality of today.
- We must be careful not to blame parents for these changes in the family because often they are victims of modern economic and social pressures.
- Teachers must not take over the role of parents. Our job of teaching, recognizing and strengthening the talents of our students, can in turn strengthen the family.

Where do we go from here? First we must redefine the word *family*. The American family has changed. No longer can we automatically assume a family is a happy husband and wife walking hand in hand with their two adorable children. Yes, there are still families like this, but it represents only a small percentage of all American families.

Recent studies tell us that over half of the children under 18 in the United States today will live at least part of their childhood in a single parent home. For our purposes, a family will be defined as a group of people living and growing together in community. This definition certainly includes the family above, and also single parent families, children living with grandparents or other relatives, and groups of adults living together for religious, social, or economic reasons.

After the redefinition of family has permeated our thinking, we must become sensitive to the needs of the changing family. When we talk about families we must include all the many groups that fall within the boundary of the definition. Our classroom libraries need to include children's books about non-traditional family life styles and experiences with separation and divorce.

Our spoken examples in class need to include positive remarks about one-parent families. Open House and Mother's Day letters offer us a challenge to use the broader definition of family. Not, "Children, please remember to bring your mothers and fathers to Open House," but "Please bring your families to see your work at school." Thus we have been challenged to respond to the realities of today. (Please see Activity 36.)

Living with Divorce

Because the United States has one of the highest divorce rates among the Western nations, it is very likely that your class will include children involved in divorce situations. Parents sometimes seek a teacher's advice about telling their children that they are getting a divorce. Here are some general thoughts that might be helpful if your advice is requested.

- Before discussing a divorce with children, make sure the decision is irrevocable. It is cruel to tease children with the threat of divorce. However, if the divorce is imminent, experts agree that it is best to tell the children at once.
- The discussion should not take place after a heated argument.
- If possible, both parents should be present.
- Stress that both parents are interested in the best interests of the children.
- Stress that the children are not the reason for the divorce.
- It is best to say: "Your father and I decided that we did not want to be married any more."
- Try to avoid "Your mother and I don't love one another any more."
- Assure your child/children that parental love won't disappear after the divorce.

Emotional Reactions to Divorce

It is helpful to be familiar with and prepared for some of the emotional reactions children have to divorce.

Regression: Following a divorce, children may revert to earlier stage of development. They may feel more secure retreating to the time of safety before the breakup. Bed-wetting, thumb-sucking, or whining can be expected, especially in younger children.

Bodily Distress: A child's world has suddenly changed and attacks of anxiety can be daily. Anxiety can be accompanied by bodily change—restlessness, loss of appetite, nausea, urinary frequency, and problems with sleeping.

Hostility: Divorce threatens children with a loss of security and a loss of love. They may feel betrayed by the ones loved best and most needed. They may seek revenge. Adults tend to react by a threat of punishment. What children need at this time is understanding of feelings and reassurance of love.

Silence and Denial: Some children protect themselves from trauma by pretending the divorce didn't happen. They often talk as though their father and mother were still living together.

They may not talk about the divorce at all. If the topic is brought up, they may change the subject or leave the room.

Apparent indifference may signal problems with the reality of the divorce. It is vital that the children accept the reality of the situation, but adults must be especially patient and understanding.

Crying: Crying is a natural expression of grief and fear when security is threatened, and children are anxious about their future.

Children should not be told, "Don't cry. Everything will be all right." Children need to express feelings. Accept those feelings by saying: "Yes, I know you are going through a difficult time. I know you are crying because you care about your family."

Confusion: Children are often concerned about who will take care of them. Sometimes parents poison their chidren's attitude toward their former marriage partner. Children feel like they are in the middle. In neither household do they feel comfortable, since someone they love is under attack.

A Bill of Rights
of
Children in Divorce Actions

Judge Robert H. Hansen, of the Family Court of Milwaukee County, Wisconsin, is the author of the following Bill of Rights of Children in Divorce Actions:
I. The right to be treated as an interested and affected person and not as a pawn, possession, or chattel of either or both parents.
II. The right to grow to maturity in that home environment which will best guarantee an opportunity for the child to grow to mature and responsible citizenship.
III. The right to the day-by-day love, care, discipline, and protection of the parent having custody of the child.
IV. The right to know the non-custodial parent and to have the benefit of such parent's love and guidance through adequate visitations.
V. The right to a positive and constructive relationship with both parents, with neither parent to be permitted to degrade or downgrade the other in the mind of the child.
VI. The right to have moral and ethical values developed by precept and practices and to have limits set for behavior so that the child early in life may develop self-discipline and self-control.
VII. The right to the most adequate level of economic support that can be provided by the best efforts of both parents.
VIII. The right to the same opportunities for education that the child would have had if the family unit had not been broken.
IX. The right to periodic review of custodial arrangements and child support orders as the circumstances of the parents and the benefit of the child may require.
X. The right to recognition that children involved in a divorce are always disadvantaged parties and that the law must take affirmative steps to protect their welfare, including, where indicated, a social investigation to determine an appointment of a guardian to protect their interests.

Role of the Educator

- What then is the role of the educator? We are not marriage counselors or social workers. It is not our job to try to solve family problems. We must do what we do best—teach, love, and listen to children.
- As part of our curriculum, we must encourage children to express their feelings. They need to learn the terms: anxious, confused, frustrated, jealous, afraid, worried, tense, lonely. They can identify these feelings in their classes and religious discussions. These are universal feelings. Our children must learn that everyone experiences these feelings at some time or another. Feelings are not wrong. How we react and deal with feelings can be either positive or negative.

Books that help children express feelings can be particularly valuable during periods of heightened stress. Consider checking out some of the books suggested at the end of this chapter; they should be available from your community library.

- We must be sensitive to all the children in our class, especially when saying something like "Today everyone will make his or her mother a planter for Mother's Day." When discussing families, we must offer alternatives to the two parents, two children picture. Mother's Day and Father's Day offer a special challenge. We must use our God-given creativity to make all the children feel comfortable and accepted in our classrooms.
- When using the image of God as our loving Father or Parent, we must be careful to explain how a loving

parent acts. Unfortunately, there will be some children in our classrooms who have never known a loving, kind, and patient parent. They need to be reassured that God loves them and considers them special.

- When discussing family situations, we must be comfortable using words like stepmother, stepfather, stepbrother, and stepsister. These words are a reality to many children in our classrooms.
- Do the pictures on our bulletin boards or our teaching visual aids reflect one-parent families?
- Books alone will not make divorce easier. However, they can help sensitize adults to the needs of children, encourage communication between child and adult about feelings caused by divorce, help children of divorce recognize that their situation is not unique, and help children in intact families gain better understanding of the meaning of divorce in the lives of friends and peers.

Television, a Matter of Choice

We are part of a continuing story of salvation. Our Judeo-Christian heritage is as old as Abraham and Sarah and as current as today. Life in America presents us with an uncomfortable dichotomy between affluent living and Gospel values. Unfortunately, our story, our guide to live by, seems to fade in the midst of many temptations. Power, success, money, and television are constant persuaders to turn from our Judeo-Christian story to follow modern values.

We have 168 hours to spend each week. We have 168 hours to live our story. Unfortunately, the average American spends more time watching TV than in any other activity except sleeping. If forty-four hours each week are spent watching TV, when is there time to live our Christian story?

While we may be concerned about the effect of television on the lives of children, we would be naive to think that it does not shape our lives with equal power. Perhaps we need to evaluate the power and influence of television on our story?

- Are we alert to the sexual sterotyping of both men and women in television commercials and programming?
- Are we critical thinkers when we view commercials, news programs, and even documentaries?
- Are we conditioned into thinking that might makes right and that violence is the only successful way to resolve conflicts?
- Do we miss educational or social opportunities because it's our favorite TV night?

Television is a fact of life, a member of the family. There would be little advantage to spending pages on the evils of this "video intruder." One fact, however, cannot be overlooked—television has changed our lives. Television hasn't grown so powerful that we can't control it, but the awesome power and influence of television must be evaluated.

We all realize that television has made a dramatic impact on the lives of today's children. Let us explore how to make television our classroom ally, how to express our needs for future programing, and what resources are available to parents and teachers.

Responding Critically to Television

During the early days of television, everything was live. Now, many TV programs are taped, with anything imperfect or undesirable cut out.

Have your class review a day in their own lives as if it were a television show to be taped. Ask them to consider what happenings they would like to "shoot over again" or take out entirely. Have students use this method to evaluate their day.

Or, suggest that students pretend that they were sent here from another planet to study family life on earth. Their only way of collecting data is watching television. Have them:

- describe babies, children in school, teenagers, fathers, and mothers.
- describe a Black and Hispanic family.
- list types of family problems.
- tell how problems are solved.

Television and Families

Mobility has scattered the extended family across the United States. Most American homes don't have room for grandparents or cousins. Thus, families are left with television relatives. Unfortunately, our new relatives do all the talking, have all the adventures, and have all the answers. We can't let life pass us by. We must work to continue our salvation story.

The Christian education staff may wish to devote a meeting to the problem of having television as a family member. Perhaps a brainstorming session on alternatives to TV could surface valuable suggestions, such as planning low-cost parish-family outings or family social action projects.

Is it possible for families to rediscover conversation, reading, sports activities, family walks, and celebrating? Can we learn to put television into its proper place? Can we stop planning family meals, Thanksgiving, and Christmas dinners around televised sports activities? Suggest that the children share some of these ideas with their families.

- Go on a TV diet.
- Plan two nights a week with the TV off. Choose family activites that can be done together.
- Put the TV in a little-used room.
- When TV is watched, be selective. You don't put

garbage in your mouth, so don't put it in your brain.

• Never use the TV as a baby sitter.

Encourage the students to read *A Kids' TV Guide,* by Joy Wilt (Word). This book teaches wise program selection and discusses how to evaluate tempting commercials.

Keep informed about special programs. Plan to use quality shows as a a supplement to present curriculum. Handouts for parents can encourage them to watch TV with their children and evaluate the presentations.

Coping with Advertising

Commercials are an inescapable part of television. The average child sees over 20,000 commercials each year and almost every parent has had to deal with a request to buy a product their child has seen advertised on television. Critics have challenged the basic fairness of advertising to children. Children must learn to evaluate commercials.

1. First, children need to understand the difference between a program and a commercial. Studies have found that the majority of children under eight have difficulty explaining the difference.

• Ask children what is on the screen.
• If it is a commercial, ask, "What is it trying to sell?"

2. Commercial follow-through:

• First, ask students to pay close attention to TV advertisements and record all the information they can about a certain toy or product.
• Next, have the students find a newspaper advertisement of the product.
• Lastly, encourage the students to go to a store and examine the product.

After all the data has been collected, the students can evaluate the advertisements.

3. Locating tricky techniques: Often commercials are elaborate creations. Making children aware of these techniques can help them evaluate the appeals made in TV commercials. Students must become familiar with such terms as camera angle, dramatic lighting, fast cutting.

4. Here are some good questions for students to ask before buying a game or advertised toy:

• Will the toy work? Will it do what the commercial says?
• Is the toy safe?
• Can I use the toy by myself, or will I need a lot of help from an adult?
• How long will it last?
• Will this toy stimulate my thinking, my creativity, or my physical activity?
• Is this toy something I really need to make me happy?
• Is it worth the money?

(Please see Activities 37, 38, and 39.)

Television Anonymous

The following letter was sent to the parents of a fourth-grade class. It may help students to be decision-makers and help solve the problem of television overkill.

Dear Parents:

Here are some basic facts, opinions, and solutions for your consideration:

Fact 1: There are 8,760 hours in one year.
Fact 2: Your child spends 850 hours in school each year.
Fact 3: If you subtract school time, sleeping time, and eating time, you are left with about 4,500 hours.
Fact 4: Unfortunately, almost half of that free time is spent in front of the television.
Fact 5: That means TV time equals almost three times the amount of time your child is in school.
Fact 6: Thus, your child spends more time watching game shows, rock stars, murders, attacks, and cartoons than he or she does reading books, computing math problems, jumping rope, or doing science experiments.
Opinion: This is a sad situation.
Solution: The fourth grade has a new club. Your child _____(name) has volunteered to be a member of this club.
Club Name: TELEVISION ANONYMOUS CLUB (T.A.C.)
Club Objectives:
1. To help children to be wise decision-makers.
2. To encourage children to use free time in a creative, active way.
Club Rules:
1. TV is to be regarded as ONE way to spend free time, not the only way.
2. TV viewing is to be kept at a minimum: for example, one hour after school and one hour after dinner.
3. We will learn to select shows we want to watch. Is there some reason why we want to sit down and spend our time watching this particular show? We must make wise decisions.
4. An exception to Rule 2 would be specials that are educational, sports events on weekends, and news programs.
5. We will fill out a paper each night listing the TV shows we watched and then list how we spent our free time. We will evaluate our papers together.
6. The T.A.C. will meet and select alternative activities. Example: reading a book; writing and illustrating a story; an art project; playing a game with the family; household jobs; playing a musical instrument.

WE NEED YOUR HELP! Television withdrawal may be painful at first. Children need encouragement to redirect their free-time patterns.

Good Books About Families and Divorce

PRESCHOOL AND PRIMARY GRADES

All Kinds of Families, by Norma Simon (A. Whitman).

The Boy with a Problem, by Joan Fassler (Human Science Press).

Eliza's Daddy, by Ianthe Thomas (Harcourt, Brace, Jovanovich).

Emily and the Klunky Baby and the Next-Door Dog, by Joan Lexau (Dial).

A Father Like That, by Charlotte Zolotow (Harper and Row).

A Friend Can Help, by Terry Berger (Raintree Publishers).

Friday Night Is Papa Night, by Ruth Sonneborn (Viking).

How Do I Feel?, by Norma Simon (A. Whitman).

I Won't Go Without a Father, by Muriel Stanek (Whitman).

Jenny's Revenge, by Anne Morris Baldwin (Four Winds Press).

Joshua's Day, by Sandra Surowiecki (Lollipop Power).

Martin's Father, by Mergrit Eichler (Lollipop Power).

Me Day, by Joan Lexau (Dial).

Where Is Daddy? The Story of a Divorce, by Beth Goff (Beacon Press).

INTERMEDIATE GRADES

The Animal, Vegetables, and John D. Jones, by Betsy Byars (Yearling).

The Divorce Express, by Paula Danziger (Dell).

It's Not the End of the World, by Judy Blume (Bradbury Press).

Johnny May, by Robbie Branscum (Doubleday).

My Dad Lives In a Downtown Hotel, by Peggy Mann (Scholastic).

A Month of Sundays, by Rose Blue (Watts).

Nobody Has to Be a Kid Forever, by Hila Colman (Crown).

A Private Matter, by Kathryn Ewing (Scholastic).

Stepchild, by Terry Berger (Messner).

To Live a Lie, by Anne Alexander (Atheneum).

Tuff Stuff, by Joy Wilt (Word).

UPPER GRADES

The Boys and Girls Book About Divorce, by Richard Gardner (Bantam). Gardner stresses two points: divorce doesn't reflect on the self-worth of a child, and a child isn't alone in his or her feelings and reactions about divorce.

Explaining Divorce to Children, edited by Earl A. Grollman (Beacon).

A Kid's Book of Divorce By, For, and About Kids, edited by Eric E. Rofes (Random House).

On Divorce, by Sara B. Stein (Walker).

Talking About Divorce, A Dialogue Between Parent and Child, by Earl A. Grollman (Beacon). One section each for children and parents. Book aims to guide parents and children toward understanding the meaning of divorce and encourage communication.

Where Do I Belong? A Kid's Guide to Stepfamilies, by Bradley Addison (Wesley).

Resources

Networks
ABC-TV
1330 Avenue of the Americas
New York, N.Y. 10019

CBS Television Network
51 W. 52nd Street
New York, N.Y. 10020

NBC-TV
30 Rockefeller Plaza
New York, N.Y. 10020

Public Broadcasting Service
475 L'Enfant Plaza West, S.W.
Washington, D.C. 20024

Government Regulatory Agencies
Federal Communications Commission
Consumer Assistance Office
1919 M St., N.W.
Washington, D.C. 20054
(The FCC licenses television stations and is responsible
for broadcast stations' general programming and
advertising policies.)

Federal Trade Commission
Bureau of Consumer Protection
Pennsylvania Ave. and 6th St., N.W.
Washington, D.C. 20580
(The FTC regulates advertising and is concerned with
specific commercials that may be deceptive or unfair.)

*The Family Guide to Children's Television—What to Watch,
What to Miss, What to Change and How to Do It,* by
Evelyn Kaye (Pantheon Books).

How to Talk Back to Your Television Set, by Nicholas
Johnson (Little, Brown & Co.).

The Incredible Television Machine, by Lee Polk and Eda
LeShan (Macmillan).

*Television and Growing Up: The Impact of Television
Violence,* A Report to the Surgeon General (U.S.
Printing Office).

Television and Society, by Harry J. Skornis (McGraw-
Hill).

Television in the Lives of Our Children, by Schramm,
Lyle, and Parker (Stanford University Press).

What's On Tonight?, by James Brieg (Liguori
Publications).

Support Groups
ACT Quarterly (newsletter), 46 Austin Street,
Newtonville, Mass. 02160.
Better Radio and Television. P.O. Box 43640, Los
Angeles, Calif. 90043.
National Association for Better Broadcasting. 373 N.
Western Ave., Los Angeles, Calif. 90004.
National Citizen's Committee for Broadcasting. 1028
Connecticut Ave., Washington, D.C. 21136. They
periodically publish lists of the most violent and least
violent programs and sponsors of these programs.
Project Focus Newsletter, edited by Shirley A.
Lieberman. Clarifies role, place, and impact of TV in
our lives. *Viewsletter,* published September to June
$3.25. For sample copy, write: 1061 Brook Ave., St.
Paul, Minn. 55113.

The American Family

By _____

1. What does the word "family" mean? _____
   _____

2. Describe your family. _____
   _____
   _____
   _____
   _____

3. What activities does your family like to do together? _____
   _____

4. My family is great because _____
   _____

5. I wish my family _____
   _____

6. Sometimes my family _____
   _____

7. The biggest problem facing American families is _____
   _____

Commercial Journal

By _____

The following commercials were shown during one hour of television.

	Date	Time

1. _____ _____
2. _____ _____
3. _____ _____
4. _____ _____
5. _____ _____
6. _____ _____
7. _____ _____

8. _____ _____
9. _____ _____
10. _____ _____
11. _____ _____
12. _____ _____
13. _____ _____
14. _____ _____

Put a star in front of the commercials you found misleading.

Put a square in front of the commercials you thought were offensive.

I think television commercials could be improved by _____

_____

How many of the commercials began with a man speaking? _____

How many of the commercials ended with a man speaking? _____

What sexual stereotypes were evident in the commercials? _____

_____

What commercial did you like best? Why? _____

_____

What commercial did you like least? Why? _____

_____

Being a Wise Consumer

By _____

Recently I bought/received _____

The toy cost _____ at _____
                                          place of purchase

Is the toy safe? _____

How long will it last? _____

How will this toy stimulate my thinking and creativity? _____

_____

Was the toy worth the money? Why? _____

_____

Will the toy work? _____

Will it do what the commercial or advertising says? _____

Is this toy something I really need to make me happy? _____

Why? _____

_____

I first heard about this toy from _____

Would you tell a friend to buy this toy? Why? _____

_____

A Commercial for Peace

By _____

Setting: _____

Characters: _____

Opening Statement: _____

Brief Outline of Main Concepts: _____

_____

_____

Musical Background: _____

Closing Statement: _____

_____

_____

_____

Please plan to present this commercial to your classmates.

CHAPTER SEVEN

Save Our Earth

Our planet is divided into almost 150 sovereign nations. These countries have real differences, yet all are united by a fabric of common needs—food, clean air, clean water, manufactured goods, jobs and income, and hope for the future. Chapter Seven explores the need to "Save Our Earth."

Dear God . . .
Help us to open our eyes and hearts to the message of Chief Seattle. Help us to learn to respect our earth, our gift from you. Help us to see the beauty around us and its need for preservation.

Help us to open our eyes to the dangers that now surround us. Help us to see the results of polluted air and water. Help us to see the hungry and cold people in our neighborhoods. Help us to acknowledge the plight of the Third World people. Help us to see through advertisements that scream at us "to carry clout," to purchase another car, to smoke another cigarette, to buy another toy. Help us to discover the difference between a *want* and a *need*.

And, Lord, after we have seen, help us to do. Help us to develop a lifestyle of simple living, to make a conscious effort to preserve our resources. Help us to reach out to those in need in our own neighborhoods. Help us to support world-wide relief projects and the redistribution of

power and resources for the future. Help us to realize when "enough is enough." Help us to refuse the high-pressure advertising campaigns and look again at our buying habits.

It will not be easy, dear God, since changes are often painful. It won't be easy to examine our lifestyles truthfully and admit our failings. We will need your help, our God, and the support of our families and friends.

Dear God, we have much to be thankful for, but we still have much to do. Help us to use the gifts of creation as they were intended, to be shared by all.

Dear God, this is a time of Thanksgiving. Help us to use our talents to preserve your gifts to us. Help us to turn away from material goods and simplify our lifestyles and turn back to you. Chief Seattle was right, you are the same God. This earth is precious to you. We are brothers and sisters, after all.

The Message of Chief Seattle

Chief Seattle, leader of the Suquamish tribe in the Washington territory, delivered a prophetic speech in 1854 while making the transferral of ancestral Indian lands to the federal government. (Please see Activity 40.) This is an adaptation of his remarks, based on an English translation by William Arrowsmith.

The Great Chief in Washington sends word that he wishes to buy our land. The Great Chief also sends us words of friendship and good will. This is kind of him since we know he has little need of our friendship in return. But we will consider your offer, for we know that if we do not sell, the white man may come with guns and take our land.

How can you buy or sell the sky, the warmth of the land? The idea is strange to us. If we do not own the freshness of the air and the sparkle of the water, how can you buy them? Every part of this earth is sacred to my people. Every shining pine needle, every sandy shore, every mist in the dark woods, every clearing, and humming insect is holy in the memory and experience of my people. The sap which courses through the trees carries the memories of the red man.

The white man's dead forget the country of their birth when they go to walk among the stars. Our dead never forget this beautiful earth, for it is the mother of the red man. We are part of the earth and it is part of us. The perfumed flowers are our sisters; the deer, the horse, the great eagle, these are our brothers. The rocky crests, the juices in the meadows, the body heat of the pony, and man, all belong to the same family.

So, when the Great Chief in Washington sends word that he wishes to buy our land, he asks much of us. The Great Chief sends word he will reserve us a place so that we can live comfortably to ourselves. He will be our father and we will be his children. So we will consider your offer to buy our land. But it will not be easy, for this land is sacred to us.

This shining water that moves in the streams and rivers is not just water but the blood of our ancestors. If we sell you land, you must remember that it is sacred and you must teach your children that it is sacred and that each ghostly reflection in the clear water of the lakes tells of events and memories in the life of my people. The water's murmur is the voice of my father's father. The rivers are our brothers, they quench our thirst. The rivers carry our canoes and feed our children. If we sell you our land, you must remember, and teach your children, that the rivers are our brothes, and yours, and you must henceforth give the rivers the kindness you would give any brother.

The red man has always retreated before the advancing white man, as the mist of the mountain runs before the morning sun. But the ashes of our fathers are sacred. Their graves are holy ground, and so these hills, these trees, this portion of the earth is consecrated to us. We know that the white man does not understand our ways. One portion of land is the same to him as the next, for he is a stranger who comes in the night and takes from the land whatever he needs. The earth is not his brother, but his enemy, and when he has conquered it, he moves on. He leaves his father's graves behind, and he does not care. He kidnaps the earth from his children. He does not care. His father's graves and his children's birthright are forgotten. He treats his mother, the earth, and his brother, the sky, as things to be bought, plundered, sold like sheep or bright beads. His appetite will devour the earth and leave behind only a desert.

I do not know. Our ways are different from your ways. The sight of your cities pains the eyes of the red man. But perhaps it is because the red man is a savage and does not understand. There is no quiet place in the white man's cities. No place to hear the unfurling of leaves in spring or the rustle of insect's wings. But perhaps it is because I am a savage and do not understand. The clatter only seems to insult the ears. And what is there to life if a man cannot hear the lonely cry of the whippoorwill or the arguments of the frogs around a pond at night? I am a red man and do not understand. The Indian prefers the soft sound of the wind itself, cleansed by a midday rain, or scented with the piñon pine.

The air is precious to the red man, for all things share the same breath, the beast, the tree, the man, they all share the same breath. The white man does not seem to notice the air he breathes. Like a man dying for many days, he is numb to the stench. But if we sell you our land, you must remember that the air is precious to us, that the air shares its spirit with all the life it supports. The wind that gave our grandfather his first breath also receives his last sigh. And the wind must also give our children the spirit of life. And if we sell you our land, you must keep it apart and sacred, as a place where even the white man can go to taste the wind that is sweetened by the meadow's flowers.

So we will consider your offer to buy our land. If we decide to accept, I will make one condition: the white man must treat the beasts of this land as his brothers. I am a savage and I do not understand any other way. I have seen a thousand rotting buffaloes on the prairie, left by the white man who shot them from a passing train. I am a savage and I do not understand how the smoking iron horse can be more important than the buffalo that we kill only to stay alive. What is man without the beasts? If all the beasts were gone, men would die from a great loneliness of spirit. For whatever happens to the beasts, soon happens to man. All things are connected.

You must teach your children that the ground beneath their feet is the ashes of our grandfathers. So that they will respect the land, tell your children that the earth is rich with the lives of our kin. Teach your children what we have taught our children, that the earth is our mother. Whatever befalls the earth, befalls the sons of the earth. If men spit upon the ground, they spit upon themselves. This we know. The earth does not belong to man, man belongs to the earth. This we know. All things are connected like the blood which unites one family. All things are connected. Whatever befalls the earth befalls the sons of the earth. Man did not weave the web of life, he is merely a strand in it. Whatever he does to the web, he does to himself.

But we will consider your offer to go to the reservation you have for my people. We will live apart, and in peace. It matters little where we spend the rest of our days. Our children have seen their fathers humbled in defeat. Our warriors have felt shame, and after defeat they turn their days in idleness and contaminate their bodies with sweet foods and strong drink. It matters little where we pass the rest of our days. They are not many. A few more hours, a few more winters, and none of the children of the great tribes that once lived on this earth or that roam now in small bands in the woods will be left to mourn the passing of my people. But why should I mourn the passing of my people? Tribes are made of men, nothing more. Men come and go, like the waves of the sea.

Even the white man, whose God walks and talks with him as friend to friend, cannot be exempt from the common destiny. We may be brothers after all, we shall see. One thing we know, which the white man may one day discover—our God is the same God. You may think now that you own Him as you wish to own our land, but you cannot. He is the God of man, and His compassion is equal for the red man and the white. This earth is precious to Him, and to harm the earth is to heap contempt on its Creator. The whites too shall pass, perhaps sooner than all other tribes. Continue to contaminate your bed, and you will one night suffocate in your own waste.

But in your perishing you will shine brightly, fired by the strength of the God who brought you to this land and for some special purpose gave you dominion over this land and over the red man. This destiny is a mystery to us, for we do not understand when the buffalo are all slaughtered, the wild horses are tamed, the secret corners of the forest heavy with the scent of many men, and the view of the ripe hills blotted by talking wires. Where is the thicket? Gone. Where is the eagle? Gone. And what is it to say goodbye to the swift pony and the hunt? The end of living and the beginning of survival.

So we will consider your offer to buy our land. If we agree, it will be to secure the reservation you have promised. There, perhaps, we may live out our brief days as we wish. When the last red man has vanished from this earth, and his memory is only the shadow of a cloud moving across the prairie, these shores and forests will still hold the spirits of my people. For they love this earth as the newborn loves its mother's heartbeat. So if we sell you our land, love it as we have loved it. Care for it as we have cared for it. Hold in your mind the memory of the land as it is when you take it. And with all your strength, with all your mind, with all your heart, preserve it for your children, and love it—as God loves us all.

One thing we know. Our God is the same God. This earth is precious to Him. Even the white man cannot be exempt from the common destiny. We may be brothers after all. We shall see.

Looking Around

We need a commitment to a simpler lifestyle. What material possessions do we really need? Do we really need that new dress or new pair of shoes? Is it possible to fix things instead of throwing them away and buying new ones? Do we recycle items instead of throwing them into the garbage? (Please see Activities 41, 44, 46, 47, 48, 49, 50, 51.)

Your Christian education staff can meet and brainstorm ways to be more saving. Some possibilities are car pooling, cooperative shopping, a classroom non-waste policy, mutual responsibility for keeping the building and grounds clean.

Sometimes we give our classes little treats. Many of our children don't need that extra sweet or trinket that is soon lost or destroyed. Why not put your treat money in a special fund. Use the $5.00 or so to donate to a worthy cause in the name of your class. The students feel good about giving and they get involved. Have the students suggest who should get the money and why. Students need to be encouraged to make decisions about giving, because often they don't have the opportunity to give because they don't have any money and aren't encouraged to see themselves as givers as well as receivers.

Does our classroom celebrate the gifts of God's creation? Do we have plants that students learn to love and water? Do we have displays of rocks and shells? Are there special places for leaves and seeds?

Is there a bird feeder outside the classroom window? If not, roll a pine cone in peanut butter and bird seed and hang it from a tree for our feathered friends. Students need nature in the classroom.

Gondwana Day

Gondwana is the world's newest nation. It is also the largest and the most populous. You won't find its borders marked on even the most up-to-date maps, because Gondwana has no frontiers.

Gondwana is the geologist's name for the single global continent in which all the world's land mass was united billions of years ago. And though that continent broke apart long before the evolution of humanity, it has recently been "reborn" in a very important sense. (Please see Activity 45.)

It is true that our planet is still divided into almost 150 sovereign countries. These countries have wide and real differences. Yet all these countries are united by a fabric of common needs—needs that cannot be met in self-centered isolaton or unrestrained competition. As a result, whatever our nationality, we are all "citizens" of the new Gondwana. For example:

- We all need to eat, yet no country is entirely self-sufficient.
- We all need hundreds of manufactured items, yet how many countries have the industrial capacity, let alone the raw materials, to fullfill this need on their own?
- We all need jobs and incomes yet national economies are linked in a worldwide web.
- We all need clean air and pure water, yet no country can protect its atmosphere or rainfall from pollution far beyond its own borders.
- We all need hope for the future, yet the arsenals of the world contain the equivalent of 30,000 pounds of TNT for every man, woman, and child on this planet.

We must work together. We must see the world as a reconstituted Gondwana.

Gondwana Day Ideas

Discuss:

- What does it mean to be a world citizen?
- How does the term Gondwana apply to us?
- How do we depend upon other countries?
- How does an event in the Near East or Central America affect our economy?
- How can we help conserve our world's natural resources?

Have students design their own Gondwana symbol, or use the symbol shown below. You can trace the design on a ditto and give each child a copy to decorate and wear on Gondwana Day.

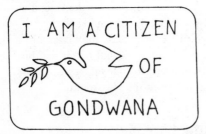

Have Students Look Around . . .

- Look at the community. Have the students study it as if they were seeing it for the first time. List things that need to be changed and things that don't.

- Make a scrapbook about the community.
- Design a perfect environment for the community. Make a drawing or model.
- How have homes changed? Why have they changed? Contrast the style, size, and building materials in older houses with those being built today. What has caused the design of houses to change?
- Homes of the future will need to use less energy. How can this be done? What has caused these changes? What effect will an energy shortage have on life styles of future generations?
- Identify problems involving soil, water, air, and plant life in the community, and suggest and defend possible solutions to the problems.
- Discuss the concept that the earth is a spaceship with limited resources and has a limited capacity for recycling.
- Explore how animals use materials from the environment in building homes.

Things to Do

Pick one resource in your area (timber, water, etc.). List all the jobs that depend upon that resource. What would happen to these jobs if the resource were destroyed?

Make a survey. Find out if people would be willing to buy less attractive fruit and vegetables if they knew growers would not use pesticides and inorganic fertilizers. Report your findings to the class.

Find out which animals contribute to the economy of your community and your state.

Learn about the programs of some organizations in your community and state whose main purpose is to preserve birds and other wildlife.

Learn under what conditions animals in your state have become extinct or endangered. What can be done to prevent this?

Identify four individuals who have worked diligently to improve the environment in your community and express appreciation of their efforts by writing or visiting them.

Have students estimate the cost of a year's supply of water if water costs 10¢ per gallon.

Plan and participate in collection campaigns which will help in the recycling of waste. Organize your own recycling project.

Discuss why humanity must abandon its "use and move on" practices.

Students need to discuss the Native American's view of our earth. For older students, you might use the message of Chief Seattle.

Here are some good books to read to children or for children to read to themselves:

- *Everybody Needs a Rock,* by Byrd Baylor (C. Scribners).
- *Hawk, I'm Your Brother,* by Byrd Baylor (C. Scribners).

- *The Trees Stand Shining: Poetry of the North American Indians,* selected by Hettie Jones (Dial Press).

Encourage the students to invite a lonely neighbor or someone from a local nursing home to Thanksgiving dinner. Make Thanksgiving an act of faith and service. "Whatsoever you do to the least of my brothers, That you do unto me."

For homework, assign a nature treasure hunt. Some examples of items they might search for are:

- a white rock
- something orange
- a berry
- address of animal shelter
- a leaf rubbing
- something that floats
- a grey hair
- a seed

Hunger

(Please see Activities 42 and 43.)

Plan a community soup and bread meal featuring homemade dark bread, no butter, and thin soup. One or more of the following activities could be the program following the meal. Some of the activities are appropriate for classroom use.

Explore an alternate diet.

- Keep track of what we eat for a week.
- Compare our diet to the diet of the world's starving peoples.
- Determine the vast amount of waste.
- Consider what our response should be. Perhaps we could find ways to share food or plan to help hungry children?

Examine our own diets. Do we need large amounts of meat? Do we need to eat meat every day? How can we make sure we are getting enough protein without relying on meat? How do meatless meals help solve the global problems?

Write a recipe book with meatless dishes. The children will find that there are many, and perhaps the book could be reproduced and taken home.

Learn the food chain. Define the relationship between global hunger and the way we now live. Consumption of goods is related to global hunger, so we first have to ask about our patterns of living. What do we buy? Where do we buy it? How do we use it?

Read food labels. Become informed consumers.

Learn where people are hungry. Find out what countries currently face the most serious food shortages. Find those countries on a map or globe.

Read newspapers and magazines and watch T.V. Know the needy areas of the world.

Find out who is hungry in your neighborhood and why.

Write your congressmen. Ask what they feel about hunger issues, what they are doing to sponsor or support concrete legislation in favor of the hungry world.

Read the gospels together. Talk about what Jesus' message of poverty and simplicity means for us today.

Offer your help. Each city or town has special groups that help people in need, such as Northwest Pilot Project, FISH, Francis Center, and so on. Why not call and see if your class can be of some assistance? For example: making Thanksgiving cards for shut-ins, small treat baskets, or a short program for Loaves and Fishes.

Plan a special liturgy. The liturgy might be planned with the theme of helping the world's hungry. A food collection might be used as part of the offertory procession and the "fruits of the harvest" might be donated to a local food relief or charity kitchen.

During Advent sponsor a parish-wide meatless potluck dinner. Every person or family would bring a meatless dish and the recipe. The recipes could then be collected and printed for those interested.

Good Books About Saving Our Earth

Child of the Dark, by Carolina Maria de Jesus (New American Library). Describes the misery and hopelessness of life in a city slum.

Feeding the World of the Future, by Hal Hellman (M. Evans & Co.).

A Handful of Rice, by Kamal Harkandaya (Fawcett). Describes the precarious existence of an Indian family.

This Hungry World, by Elizabeth Helfman (Lothrop, Lee & Shepard Co.).

Resources

Bread for the World, by Arthur Simon (Paulist Press). An action guide published by the organization Bread for the World. It is available for $1.50 from Paulist Press, 400 Sette Drive, Paramus, N.J. 07652.

By Bread Alone, by Lester Brown, offers the latest compilation of interesting data on the world food problem.

New Hope for the Hungry, by Larry Minear, a 140-page paperback, is available for $1.95 from Friendship Press, 475 Riverside Dr., New York, N.Y. 10027.

Recipes for a Small Planet, by Ellen Ewald (Ballantine Books). Suggests ways of serving less meat and more protein.

Who Shall Eat? available from AFSC, 15 Rutherford Pl., New York, N.Y. 10003, for $1.00, is a good resource for teachers. This pamphlet sets forth central questions related to the world food situation and gives summaries of solutions and values involved.

It is important that children see themselves as citizens of the world. They also need to place themselves in time and space. A song that easily teaches both concepts is "We All Live Together" from the *We All Live Together Album /1.* (There are also Volumes 2, 3 and 4, and the records are worth the money.) The records address basic skills, rhythm and movement, sing-a-long songs, call and response, creative play, resting, etc. From Youngheart Music Education Service, Los Angeles, California, 1978.

Teacher Kits

The Hunger Kit, available from the Program of Studies in Peace and Human Development, St. Joseph's College, 54th and City Line Avenue, Philadelphia, Penn. 19131, for $1.50, contains reference and informational materials focused on two major areas of world hunger—problems in developing nations and domestic responses to them. Incorporates a special appeal from religious and biblical aspects.

Hunger on Spaceship Earth, available from the American Friends Service Committee, 15 Rutherford Place, New York, N.Y. 10003, $2.00, includes background readings, action ideas, global ramifications, and a simulation for classroom use.

The Needs of Man, available from Zen-Du Products, P. O. Box 3927, Hayward, Calif. 94540, $1.25, for intermediate and middle school teachers, is a brightly colored wheel device that correlates human needs such as food, social institutions, and interdependence with suggested project activities.

Peace Studies Packet, available from Robert Ribsley, The Christophers, 12 West 48th St., New York, N.Y. 10017, at no charge, contains course outline, bibliographies,

resource lists, and information pamphlets.

Teaching About World Hunger, available from U.S. Comm. for UNICEF, 331 East 38th Street, New York, N.Y. 10016, order No. 5419, $2.00, surveys world hunger and the interdependent factors affecting world food supplies. Includes readings, wall-sheet, posters, and charts showing food consumption and protein conversions, guide and bibliography. Secondary school teachers, check this one.

The following three items are available from Franciscan Communications, 1229 S. Santee St., Los Angeles, Calif. 90015:

The Empty Place, a family activity book, one to ninety-nine copies @ 60¢, 100-199 @ 57¢.

Feed My Lambs, a parish program on world hunger and hope. The first four copies are free: 25¢ for each additional copy.

Responses to World Hunger, 33" × 44" poster, graphically shows activities to help overcome hunger, for individuals and groups. Price: one to five @ $1.00, six to twenty-five @ $.80.

McDonald's publishes an *Ecology and Energy Action Pack.* This well-written unit has ditto masters and overhead transparencies and a variety of good ideas. If you are interested, send $2.00 to McDonald's Action Packs, Box 2594, Chicago, Ill. 60690, and ask for the pack on Ecology and Energy.

PROJECT JONAH will send you a kit with a book of stories and activities about whales and what you can do to help them. Write PROJECT JONAH, Box 476, Bolinas, Calif. 94924.

These books are offered by The Institute for Peace and Justice, 2747 Rutger St., St. Louis, Mo. 63104.

Bread and Justice: Teacher's Manual by James B. McGinnis. Provides additional background information to textbooks as well as step-by-step lesson plans and ideas for projects. Also lists additional resources, AV's, etc. $7.95 (includes mailing).

Bread and Justice: Toward a New International Economic Order, by James B. McGinnis. Textbook for education purposes, pinpointing the economic cause of world hunger and ways for individuals to act to change the economic and political structure which contributes to hunger. $5.95 (includes mailing).

Those Who Hunger, (tabloid). Lenten program for church, school, and family use, integrating social change and lifestyle change with prayer; includes Scripture readings for Lent, Lenten practices, and a variety of family activities. $1.50 (includes mailing).

Those Who Hunger: Leader's Guide. Detailed instruction for conducting each of seven sessions of Lenten program providing additional information on content and activities. Variety of key quotations from Church documents are included. $7.95 (includes mailing).

Reflection: A Message

By _____

What was the message of Chief Seattle?

_____

_____

_____

_____

Why is his message of vital importance today?

_____

_____

_____

_____

How do you live the message of Chief Seattle?

_____

_____

_____

_____

Communities Adapt to Change

By _____

1. How have home designs changed in the last ten years?_____

_____

2. Why have homes changed in the last ten years?_____

_____

3. How is recycling a part of your community?_____

_____

4. Name three community members who have worked diligently to improve the environment._____

_____

_____

_____

5. Why must people change the "use and move on" practice?_____

_____

_____

6. How does your community reflect the message of Chief Seattle?_____

_____

_____

Examining My Diet

By _____

Please keep track of your dinner menu for four days.

Monday

_____

_____

_____

Tuesday

_____

_____

_____

Wednesday

_____

_____

_____

Thursday

_____

_____

_____

How many times a week did you eat meat?_____

How do meatless meals help solve the global problem of world hunger?____

_____

Read John 21:12-17. What does it tell you to do?_____

_____

_____

Facing the Hunger Problem

By _____

FACT: Today for two-thirds of the world's people, hunger is present every moment of their lives.

FACT: Twenty-five percent of all food products in North America are thrown away.

1. Is wasting food a problem in your school? _____

How do you know? What can you do about it?_____

_____

2. Is wasting food a reality at your home? _____

How do you know? What can you do about it?_____

_____

3. Name six countries that face serious food shortages.

_____   _____

_____   _____

_____   _____

4. What did Jesus mean when He said, "Come and enter the Kingdom prepared for you. For I was hungry and you gave me food; I was thirsty and you gave me drink. . . ."?_____

_____

_____

5. What is your role in helping to solve the world's hunger problem?_____

_____

_____

Peacemaker Mother Teresa

By _____

Research Mother Teresa of Calcutta and please answer the following questions.

What problems did Mother Teresa see in the world?

_____

_____

_____

What did she decide to do?

What does Mother Teresa have to say about the poor?

_____

_____

_____

How is Mother Teresa a peacemaker?

_____

_____

_____

What lesson did you learn from the example of Mother Teresa?

_____

_____

_____

Gondwana

By _____

1. What does the word "Gondwana" mean?_____

_____

_____

2. What does it mean to be a world citizen?_____

_____

_____

3. How do you depend upon other countries?_____

_____

_____

4. How does an event in Iran affect the economy of the United States?_____

_____

_____

5. How can you help conserve the world's natural resources?_____

_____

_____

Agree, Disagree, Why?

By _____

Read each of the following statements. Do you agree with the statement or disagree with the statement? In either case, please give a reason for your answer.

Food stamps should be used only to purchase food.

Agree? Disagree? Why?

_____

_____

_____

Why work when you can live it up on welfare?

Agree? Disagree? Why?

_____

_____

_____

Food, clothing, shelter, and health care are not rights of persons but are rewards for work.

Agree? Disagree? Why?

_____

_____

_____

The poor will always be with us.

Agree? Disagree? Why?

_____

_____

_____

Agree, Disagree, Why?

By _____

Read each of the following statements. Do you agree with the statement or disagree with the statement? In either case, please give a reason for your answer.

No one has a right to eat unless they work.

Agree? Disagree? Why?

_____

_____

_____

Anyone can achieve the American dream. All you have to do is work.

Agree? Disagree? Why?

_____

_____

_____

Payment should be made before the doctor will see you.

Agree? Disagree? Wny?

_____

_____

_____

People are poor because they are lazy.

Agree? Disagree? Why?

_____

_____

_____

Looking Towards the Future

By _____

The headlines of today read:

Crime Rate Rises in Cities
Bombs Explode in Northern Ireland
Thousands Die Daily in African Famine
Billions Spent on Neutron Bomb

Ten years from now, what would you like the headlines to say?

_____

_____

_____

_____

_____

What is the biggest problem that faces the world today? Why?

_____

_____

_____

What is your role in helping to solve this problem?

_____

_____

_____

United States Foreign Policy

By _____

You have been given the job to help write United States Foreign Policy. What direction would the United Sates go in the following areas?

Arms control

_____

_____

_____

Energy conservation

_____

_____

_____

Development of third world nations

_____

_____

_____

The United States and its relationship with Russia

_____

_____

_____

Share these thoughts with your representatives in Congress.

My Energy Journal

By _____

The following are the things I used today that are powered by some form of energy.

_____   _____

_____   _____

_____   _____

_____   _____

_____   _____

_____   _____

_____   _____

_____   _____

_____   _____

_____   _____

_____   _____

_____   _____

What kinds of energy did you use?

Money Talk

By _____

What does the word *poverty* mean?_____

_____

Do you know someone who is so poor that they don't have enough to eat?

_____

_____

Tell about a time when you met a person obviously poorer than you.
How did you feel?_____

_____

_____

Do you agree with the saying that "God helps those who help themselves"?
Why?_____

_____

_____

What did Jesus tell us about money?_____

_____

_____

How do you help the poor of the world?_____

_____

_____

CHAPTER EIGHT

Christmas

Christmas, a day to celebrate the birthday of the Prince of Peace. Yet, how often does the Christmas season become anything but peaceful? Is this the year to return to the real meaning of Christmas? Chapter Eight explores many ways we can celebrate the birthday of Jesus, the Prince of Peace.

Dear God . . .
Slow me down Lord. Help me to look again at the manger scene and see that I am a part of that continuing story.

Help me to take the time to look at the wonders of your creation . . .
the star-bright night
the magnificent evergreen
the smell of Christmas baking
a new born baby

Thank you God. Thank you for the gift of Your Son Jesus. Thank you for the gift of the Eucharist. Thank you for my brothers and sisters in (my city), in (my state). In Calcutta, Harlem, and Jerusalem. Thank you for creating me. May my light shine for all the world to see. May I show others the way to you and thus find the path myself.

May this Christmas season be one of peace, peace in knowing my Savior has come and will come again, peace in knowing I am loved and will love in return, peace in knowing that my love can help create a world that understands that peace is not a season, but a way of life. When the spirit of peace becomes part of our lives, every day will be Christmas, and every night will hold the promise of dawn.

Celebrating Christmas . . .

Christmas has long been a special time of year: beautifully decorated trees, caroling in the snow, the smell of freshly baked cookies, the secrets and whispers over well-planned gifts. Yes, it is an exciting time.

It seems like the few weeks between Thanksgiving and December 25 fly by in an avalanche of Christmas cards, programs, and shopping. Everthing is focused on that all-important day, Christmas. Hours are spent baking in anticipation of the "holidays." We endure traffic jams and overcrowded stores in search of that nonexistent perfect gift. Hours are spent addressing cards, decorating homes, and planning parties or family get-togethers.

The time is short, there is much to do. Baking is no longer a joy but becomes a chore that must get done, and the children are no longer invited to help, but are sent downstairs to watch TV. Program practices at schools become tedious and frustrating. Children find it hard to stand still, and teachers are burdened with unusually busy schedules. Decorating our homes is often an expensive proposition that drains our checking account.

Christmas Day finally arrives. Opening gifts at six o'clock in the morning turns the living room into a shambles. Cries of excitement are soon replaced with "Mom, the train doesn't work," and "He got ten presents and I only got eight."

Getting ready for church becomes a major event. Christmas clothes don't fit and substitutions must be made. Finally someone yells, "We are going to be late! If we aren't in the car in five minutes, we're going to be late!" Through some miracle, everyone manages to get ready. Through the service, the children are thinking of all their toys, and Mom is hoping she remembered to turn on the oven to cook the turkey and wondering where she can borrow four more folding chairs for the dinner table.

Christmas evening the children are asleep, exhausted from an emotionally charged day. Mom is relieved. At last, a few days of peace and quiet lie ahead before the round of new Year's parties. Dad secretly wonders how soon he can pay off his charge accounts for gifts that will find their way to bedroom shelves or garbage cans by February 1.

While this story is exaggerated, it doesn't miss the mark by far. We set ourselves up for frustration and stress through unrealisitc expectations of ourselves, our family, and friends. Every magazine, TV commercial, and advertisement screams at us to "make this the best Christmas yet." How depressed we feel when our Christmas doesn't measure up to the expectations of a Hallmark card theology.

Alternatives

First, we need to look at what Christmas means. We must do it now, before the Christmas rush begins, because once the frantic activity has started it is very hard to stop.

Christmas is the celebration of the birth of Jesus. Advent is the time of preparation and waiting. We know that Jesus did come and our redemption has already begun, so we are a people awaiting his second coming. So when we celebrate the birthday of Jesus, we remember his message of love, his acceptance of all people, and his obedience to God.

If we truly understand the meaning of Christmas, our celebration must reflect it. We need to sit down and quietly examine our patterns of celebrating Christmas.

Invite the children to join you in a discussion on how can we make the season joyful yet peaceful; rich in traditions, yet emphasizing a simple life style; fun, yet keeping with the gospel message of sharing? Here are some suggestions.

- We must treasure and appreciate each day. While December 25 is important, so is November 28, December 5, and December 17. Baking must be enjoyed for its own value, not just to have sweets for the holidays. The holiday is today. The time spent with family and friends is just as important now as on Christmas Day.

A word of caution about Christmas programs: we must remember that the process is as important as the end product. What pains we often put children through for the sake of a forty-minute program that no one remembers a month later! But the children remember. Their Christmas season may have been marked by the impatience and harsh words of an adult who was frustrated by unrealistic expectations. A Christmas program should be a joyful experience that helps children feel that they are part of a continuing story of salvation.

- List all the activities that have become Christmas "traditions." Now, put a star next to the three most important activities. How can these activities be planned so that everyone has a good time? Is it possible to share these activities with a lonely person? If there isn't time to celebrate a particular Christmas activity, can it take place during another time? It is possible to participate in many activities if we have a flexible, creative schedule.
- Christmas shopping can be a difficult experience for dispositions and pocketbooks. We need to look at our gift list. What do these people really need? How can our gifts reflect the meaning of Christmas? Is there an alternative to a blouse or shirt that will be returned on December 26, or given away before another Christmas Day dawns? How about making some of our gifts this year? How about giving gifts of time:
- A can of tennis balls and three dates to play tennis together next summer.

- Free babysitting.
- Tutoring a child having difficulties in school.
- Chopping and stacking wood for the winter.

We might also consider alternative gift-giving:

- A certificate saying a poor child has received a new pair of shoes.
- A donation to a charity in the name of the person.
- Another alternative to traditional gift-giving could be a return to the Twelve Days of Christmas. When children are besieged with so many gifts at one time, they are often confused. They long to really look at the gift and play with it. There simply isn't time when they are urged to keep opening the other gifts. At the other extreme, we have the child who tears open every present only to ask, "Is that all?" Either way we are doing a disservice to children. We all need time to appreciate a gift given to us, use it, and say "Thank you." Why not celebrate the Twelve Days of Christmas and extend the gift-giving time? Why do all gifts have to be given on or by Christmas Day? There are several days during the Twelve of Christmas that are appropriate for gift-giving.
- As Christians we have a special message to share: Christ's birth, resurrection, and return. Christ left us his legacy of love. Have we taken the time to share this with one another? Have we shared our time with lonely people in nursing homes or retirement complexes?

We must resist the urge to over-prepare and over-celebrate. When we set our priorities straight, we can enjoy each moment and celebrate each day. Then we can awaken on December 26 without the feeling that we missed Christmas, that somehow it got lost in the shuffle.

Peace is not a season . . . it is a way of life. When the Spirit of Peace becomes a part of our lives, every day will be Christmas, and every night will hold the promise of dawn.   Author Unknown
     (Please see Activity 53.)

Advent Ideas

List and discuss with your class the times when we wait: in line on a freeway, for dinner, to get over being angry, to go to recess, for a friend to come over, in line at the store. (Please see Activity 52.)
     Then discuss:

- What do you think about when you are waiting?
- What do you learn about yourself from waiting?
- How can we grow to be better persons from waiting?
- What do patience and hope mean?
- Why do you think waiting is part of our life?
- How would life be different if we never had to wait?

- What does this mean: "Your patience with your brothers and sisters is a sure sign of your love for them"?
- Describe someone you think is a patient person.
- Make up a prayer asking God to help each of your family members to be patient in some special way.
- Why is Christmas worth waiting for?

The Jesse Tree

This well-known Advent activity could be used with a new objective. As well as decorating a paper Christmas tree with symbols of Old Testament people waiting for the coming of the Savior (Noah's ark, Joseph's coat of many colors, Joseph's carpenter tools, David's harp) you might also add symbols of contemporary people waiting for Jesus' second conimg (people in our classroom, well-known people).

ADVENT ANGELS: A beautiful Advent custom that has been tried successfully in many families is the Advent angel. You may celebrate this custom in your classroom or home. On the first few days of Advent participants gather and each picks a slip of paper out of a hat telling whom they will be an Advent angel to.

Each person then becomes the angel for the person whose name they have drawn. Simple acts of kindness may be performed, such as household tasks, a note of encouragement, a small gift. This is all to be done in secret, though the angels may work together to help one another. On Christmas Eve the angels give their special person a small gift with their names enclosed, thus disclosing their identity.

An Epiphany Liturgy

Introduction:
Christmas is a time for gifts. We all love to receive gifts and give gifts to others. Today we will take time to celebrate our three greatest presents: the gift of creation, the Birth of our Savior, and the gift of Holy Communion.

Opening Song: "Prepare Ye the Way of the Lord" (or song about preparation)

Penitential Rite:
Response: Jesus, we are sorry.

- For past Advents, when we did not watch for your coming.
- For inviting you to come to us without preparing ourselves.
- For the times we have not looked for you in others.

First Reading: 1 John 4:19-21
Response: "Day by Day" from "Godspell" (one verse)
Gospel: Matthew 3:1-3

Sermon:

Many hundreds of years ago, three wisemen followed a star in search of the newborn Savior. They finally found Jesus and knelt down and worshipped him. Then they offered him presents of gold, frankincense, and myrrh.

Jesus grew up and went from town to town teaching about God's love and faithfulness. He asked people to love his "Father in Heaven" and to "love one another" here on earth. Jesus said, "Feed the hungry. Give to the poor. Visit the lonely."

For hundreds of years, the followers of Jesus have continued to offer him gifts. But instead of gold, frankincense, and myrrh, we give the gift of ourselves. For example:

In India there is a very special person, Mother Teresa. Her gift to Jesus is her work with the poor. Everyday she helps the sick and the lonely. Her gift is worth more than gold.

In Sweden, a man dedicated his life to bringing peace to the world. His name was Dag Hammarskjöld. His gift of friendship to all nations was more valuable than frankincense.

In the United States a great man had a special dream. Martin Luther King brought the hope of unity to the people of this country. His gift was priceless.

And today and every day, people all over the world are offering their own special gifts to Jesus. So, as we remember today the gifts brought by the wise men, let us not forget our own gifts, the gifts of love that we can offer Jesus every day.

Offertory Song: "Please Accept Our Gifts" (or offering song)

Communion Song: "Oh What a Gift" (or gift-giving, sharing song)

Blessing: May Jesus be your strong friend always; and may you give to others as he gives to you.
(All) AMEN
May you have a peaceful new year;
and may your Christmas never end.
(All) AMEN
And may God bless you in the name of God the Creator, God the Savior, and God the Sanctifier.
(All) AMEN

Closing Song: "King of Glory" (or a song of celebration)

Resources

The following books for Advent are excellent resources to help us celebrate the Advent and Christmas seasons.

Advent for the Family, by Auman (Fortress Press), $1.95.

The Beggars' Christmas, by John Aurelio (Paulist Press), $3.95. Father John Aurelio is a Catholic priest who lives in Buffalo, N.Y., where he works with retarded children. His book is a fable about the true meaning of Christmas. Set in the Middle Ages, two beggars, one blind and the other crippled, encounter an animal who grants them their wish—to journey through space and time in search of the meaning of Christ's birth. The ending gives us all something to think about.

Celebrate While We Wait, Schroeder family (Concordia), $3.25.

The Christian Family Prepares for Christmas, by Mueller (Concordia), $2.25.

The Christmas Almanack, by Gerard and Patricia Del Re (Doubleday and Co.). This $7.95 book is a treasure. It covers Christmas in the Gospels, on the calendar, around the world, in music, on the page, on film.

The Family Prepares for the Messiah, by Griggs (Griggs Educational Services), $.60.

We Light the Candles, by Brandt (Augsburg), $1.25.

When All the World Was Waiting, by Woerkom (Concordia), $4.95. This Advent book for children is divided into twenty-six readings. Teachers of eight to twelve year olds will find this book an excellent way to acquaint children with the Old Testament's promises and the New Testament's fulfillment of these promises concerning the Messiah.

Advent, A Time for Waiting

By _____

1. What does the word "Advent" mean?_____

_____

2. List three times during the day when you experience waiting.

_____

_____

_____

3. What do you think about when you are waiting?_____

_____

4. What does "patience" mean?_____

_____

5. Why is Advent a time to be patient?_____

_____

_____

6. Why is Christmas worth waiting for?_____

_____

_____

Christmas

By _____

1. What does the Christmas season mean to you? _____
_____
_____

2. Why is Jesus called the Prince of Peace? _____
_____
_____

3. What is the difference between a *want* and a *need*? _____
_____
_____

4. What do you need for Christmas? _____
_____
_____

5. What do you want for Christmas? _____
_____
_____

CHAPTER NINE

A Time to Live . . .
A Time to Die . . .

Birth and death are the outside limits of human life. Within these parameters we live, produce, and grow. If Christian education is to address all aspects of a students' life—emotional, physical, and psychological—it must include a unit on death and dying. This unit centers on Lent, Holy Week, and Easter, and places death in a Christian context.

Dear God . . .
Help me to see death as my final stage of growth. Death is not my enemy; it merely sets a limit on my time in this life.

Help me to appreciate the promise of Jesus. Help me to rejoice in the hope of the Resurrection.

Help me to be aware of the special needs of the dying. May I reach out my hands in willing friendship and support.

A time to live, a time to die, belong to me. I thank you, God, for my special times, now and through eternity. Amen.

Death and Dying

The first time I taught about death in an elementary classroom, I had not planned to. One of my students had died, and we all needed to face the reality that death is a part of our human existence. That first unit was sketchy, but we all learned and shared many important ideas and feelings. For ten years I have presented a yearly unit on death and dying, since death continues to touch our lives in many ways when a beloved pet, a family member, a neighbor, a classmate, a public figure dies.

Lent offers an opportunity to examine life and death in a Christian context—to discuss, read, share, and listen together. I have found that children relate to Jesus' death more easily after exploring the idea of their own death, and Easter becomes a celebration with greater depth and meaning.

This chapter includes a short explanation about the different conceptual stages children experience in dealing with death and dying, a sample letter to parents, a list of resources and activities for the elementary students, and a sample lesson plan.

Background . . .

Psychologist Maria Nagy, who studied Hungarian children in the late 1940's, discovered three phases in children's awareness of personal mortality.

Stage One (until about age five).

Preschool children usually don't recognize that death is final, but believe it is like being less alive, or like sleep. They are still curious about what happens after death. The children want to know where and how they continue to live. Most children connect the relation of absence and funerals. But they think in the cemetery one lives on, that movement is limited by the coffin, they continue to take nourishment, to breathe, to know what is happening on earth. Death disturbs the young child because it separates people from each other and because life in the grave seems dull and unpleasant.

Stage Two (between ages five and nine).

The distinguishing characteristic of this stage is that the child now tends to personify death. Death is sometimes seen as a separate person, perhaps as an angel or a frightening clown. For other children, death is represented by a dead person. Death usually makes its rounds in the night.

The big shift in thinking from Stage One is that death is usually understood as final, not merely a reduced form of life. There is still an important protective feature here: personal death can be avoided. Run faster than the Death Man, lock the door, trick him, and you will not die unless you have bad luck. As Nagy says, "Death is still outside us and is also not general."

Stage Three (ages nine, ten and thereafter).

The oldest children in Nagy's study recognized that death is not only final but also inevitable. It will happen to them, too, no matter how fast they run or how cleverly they hide. By the time they are about nine years old, most children realize that death is final, universal, and inevitable.

Nagy's stages offer a useful guide to the development of the child's concept of death, but, of course, individual development varies.

Research indicates that adolescents' orientation toward death also fluctuates between a sense of invulnerability and a sense of impending, catastrophic doom. Some adults reveal a similar tendency to function at two levels of thought: they know that death is final and inevitable, but most of their daily attitudes and actions are more consistent with the belief that personal mortality is a myth.

Questions and Answers

Q. What do you do when a child asks, "Why do people die?"

A. When a child inquires about death, we need first to ask ourselves why he or she is asking. Often the child's most immediate need is not a long intellectual explanation but an unexpressed need for reassurance and emotional security. We might respond by saying, "Why do you ask?" After the child responds, we have a better idea of how extensive our answer needs to be.

Q. Many children worry about death. How can we reassure our children?

A. Children need our time. Often children's fears are not expressed; children worry in silence, sometimes over long periods of time. We need to take time to ask our children if they are worrying about something. Some parents show their wills to their children and let them read the provision which has been made for them in case their parents die. Knowledge helps give security. Lack of simple facts is the source of many childhood fears.

Q. A small child doesn't understand death, so I told my five year old that her grandfather just went to sleep. Right?

A. Wrong! Children deserve simple information truthfully given. Many children who are told that the dead person is just sleeping develop great fears and anxieties about going to bed. They even fight sleep for fear they won't wake up again.

Q. Do you tell even a small child about a death in the family?

A. Yes. Even a small child needs to be told the truth when a person whom he or she loves dies. We can tell the child that the person has died, that he or she still loves him or her, but that he or she cannot come back to him or her.

Q. When a child asks what death is, how do we respond?

A. Death means that your body does not work any longer—your eyes can't see, your ears can't hear, your legs can't run, your heart stops beating. Your inner self has left your body because your body could not work any more. John Quincy Adams at the age of eighty met an old friend. The friend said, "How are you today?" The ex-President replied: "John Quincy Adams is very well, thank you, but the house in which he lives is becoming dilapidated. I think John Quincy Adams will have to move out of it before very long. But he, himself, is very well, thank you." Our body is like our house here on earth. Although young children would not understand John Quincy Adams' words, they would respond to the idea, told in simpler terms.

Q. Should a child attend a funeral?

A. Generally, yes. Children need to feel that they are part of an occasion which has great meaning for the family. They may not understand all that is happening, but they know that they belong and that together we are showing our love for the person who has died. The feeling of belonging is very important to the emotional security of the child.

Q. What do you do when a pet dies?

A. The death of a pet may cause a child acute suffering. A child needs a time to grieve. A child is often helped by planning a simple service for the burial of the pet. Such a ceremony has several values: it helps the child to accept the finality of the pet's death; the loving tribute provides an outlet for feelings; and it can be an expression of the child's faith in God's love. Don't try to replace the pet immediately. It will not take the place of the one that died. After a short time, a new pet will be welcome.

A Letter to Parents

It is wise to inform your students' parents before beginning this unit. Below is a sample letter for fourth graders' parents.

Dear Parents,

Our class is beginning a unit on death and dying. This will be taught in connection with the events of Christ's last few days on earth and with an emphasis on the Resurrection.

Maria Nagy's book, *The Meaning of Death*, explains that nine and ten year olds (many for the first time) realize that death is universal and that one day they, too, will die. It is a time of many questions and confusing thoughts. Throughout this unit we will use stories, films, value games, written activities, and short services to explore this topic and its meaning to us. A panel of parents will share their own feelings and experiences with us.

The class will complete a booklet, "A Time to Live—A Time to Die," during this unit. When they bring this booklet home, please take a few minutes to discuss the book and their answers to the questions.

If you have any questions, comments, or concerns about this unit, please contact me. If you would like a copy of the unit, please check the place below and return this letter.

Yes, I would like a copy of the unit.
(Name)

Peace,

(Teacher's signature)

Parent Input

A parent panel is an effective learning experience for intermediate and junior high students. The adults should be given the questions to study in advance.

1. How do you feel about your own death?
2. What experiences have you had with death so far?
3. What is the closest you have ever come to dying? How did you feel?
4. What will happen to you after you die?
5. How would you like to die and when?
6. What would you do if you were immune to death?
7. Would you donate your body to science?
8. What would you like said about you in your obituary?
9. Do you have the right to take your own life?
10. Describe your own funeral.
11. What would you do if you had only a month left to live?

Older students could do research and then report their findings to the class. Here are some suggested report topics.

1. Is the attitude of Americans toward death substantially different from that of Europeans? Africans? Asians?
2. How is death viewed and dealt with in other cultures?
3. What are the various answers to the question, "What happens to people after death?"
4. How is death presented in popular music?
5. Is death presented differently in movies now than it used to be?
6. What are the pro and con arguments about donating your body to science?
7. Do people ever have the right to cause the death of others?
8. How does advertising exploit the fear of death?

Music

Deanna Edwards, a music therapist, has several albums of songs that have helped thousands to cope with the realities of sickness and death. Her song, "Teach Me to Die," is the theme song for Make Today Count, an organization for the terminally ill. Other excellent songs are: "Catch a Little Sunshine," "Take My Hand," and "Put My Memory in Your Pocket." Her albums, *Peacebird* and *Music, Laughter and Tears,* may be purchased in your local Christian supply centers. These records offer us yet another resource to explore the many facets of this unit.

Good Books About Death

PRESCHOOL AND PRIMARY GRADES

About Dying, by Sara Bennet Stein (Walker).

The Accident, by Carol Carrick (Clarion).

Annie and the Old One, by Miska Miles (Little, Brown).

Growing Time, by Sandol S. Warburg (Houghton Mifflin).

My Grandpa Died Today, by Joan Fassler (Human Sciences Press).

My Grandson, Lew, by Charlotte Zolotow (Harper & Row).

Nanna Upstairs and Nanna Downstairs, by Tomie De Paola (Puffin).

Stories from a Snowy Meadow, by Carla Stevens (Seabury).

The Tenth Good Thing About Barney, by Judith Viorst (Aladdin).

INTERMEDIATE GRADES

The Big Wave, by Pearl S. Buck (Scholastic).

Bridge to Terabithia, by Katherine Paterson (Avon Camelot).

The Cay, by Theodore Taylor (Avon Camelot).

Family Secrets, by Susan Shreve (Yearling).

God, Why Did He Die?, by Anne Harler (Concordia).

Grandma Didn't Wave Back, by Rose Blue (Dell Yearling).

A Taste of Blackberries, by Doris Buchanan Smith (Scholastic).

There Are Two Kinds of Terrible, by Peggy Mann (Doubleday).

Where the Lilies Bloom, by Vera and Bill Cleaver (Scholastic).

Young People Talk About Death, by Mary McHugh (Watts).

UPPER GRADES

Blew and the Death of the Mag, by Wendy Lichtman (Freestone).

By the Highway Home, by Mary Stolz (Harper & Row).

Eric, by Doris Lund (Laurel Leaf Books).

Hope for the Flowers, by Trina Paulus (Newman Press).

A Matter of Time, by Roni Schotter (Collins).

A Season In Between, by Jan Greenberg (Laurel Leaf Books).

A Summer to Die, by Louis Lowry (Bantam Books).

Tuck Everlasting, by Natalie Babbitt (Bantam Books).

ALL AGES

Another Look at the Rainbow, Center for Attitudinal Healing (Celestial Arts). Written by and for children who have brothers and sisters with a life-threatening illness.

How It Feels When a Parent Dies, by Jill Krementz (Knopf).

Straight from the Siblings: Another Look at the Rainbow (Celestial Arts).

There Is a Rainbow Behind Every Dark Cloud, edited by Gloria Murray (Celestial Arts).

Tuff Stuff, by Joy Wilt (Word, Inc.).

Teaching Suggestions for the Death Unit

Please remember to use activities you are comfortable with, consider the needs of your class, and read all books *before* you take them into the classroom.

Beginning on page 120 you will find black line masters for a student booklet called "A Time to Live and a Time to Die." The booklets are designed to complement the discussions, literature, music and prayer activities used in this unit. Permission is given by the publisher to reproduce those pages to make one booklet for each student in your classroom.

Here are some suggestions for putting this unit together.

Special needs: Primary teachers will need at least five books. Intermediate and junior high teachers will need one story for the introductory lesson (see suggestions below) and then one story to read from one class period to the other.

Week One: Introduce unit on death and dying. Read a story that only takes a short time and can be read during the class period.
Suggested reading primary:
About Dying, My Grandson Lew, Nanna Upstairs and Nanna Downstairs, The Tenth Good Thing About Barney.
Intermediate and junior high:
The Accident, Annie and the Old One, A Taste of Blackberries, Growing Time.

• Discuss story together. Children may want to share personal experiences.
• Hand out the cover page of the student booklet. Ask students to write their full name on cover. If there is time, have the children decorate the cover.
• Before the class period ends, you might want to ask students to write down any questions they want answered during the next class period.

Week Two:
• Opening Prayer
• Spend the first few minutes reading one of the stories appropriate to your level.
• Discuss.
• Hand out the first page of the student booklet. Have the students discuss their special talents and write talents in the circles on the page. Decorate.
• Hand out "When I Die" page. Have the children discuss their favorites and then complete the page. Decorate.

Week Three:
• Opening Prayer
• Spend the first few minutes reading one of the stories appropriate to your level.
• Discuss.
• Hand out the page from the student booklet, "My Feelings About Dying."
• Discuss: Feelings and Fears
How we feel about dying
What people would miss about us
Healthy Living
• Other books you might want to use during this class period might include:

How It Feels When a Parent Dies, Straight from the Siblings: Another Look at the Rainbow, There Is a

Rainbow Behind Every Dark Cloud

All contain excellent selections written by children for children. These might also be used with the lesson in the next class period.

Week Four:
• Opening Prayer
• Spend the first few minutes reading one of the stories appropriate to your grade level.
• Hand out "Last Will and Testament." What special people do we want to have our treasures?
• Teachers may use the "Epitaph" page or decide to share more selections from the books suggested in Week Three.
• This is also a good time to invite adults/parents to participate in a panel discussion. Check death unit for panel questions.

Week Five:
• Opening Prayer
• Spend the first few minutes reading one of the stories appropriate to your level.
• Hand out the "Remembering Jesus" pages from the student booklet.
• Complete the pages together and discuss each answer.
• Emphasize how Jesus felt about death and what He told us about resurrection.
• Decorate pages.
• Play records with songs about Jesus.
• Pass out parts for Lenten Celebration.

Week Six:
• Opening Prayer
• Review what we know about Jesus.
• Hand out the "Cross" page from the student booklet.
• Discuss crosses we carry.
• Participate in Lenten Celebration. (See pages 00.) • Complete Resurrection symbol page from booklet.
• Evaluate the unit.

PLEASE NOTE:
There are many ways to put this unit together. Be creative and plan what is best for you and your class.

(sample booklet pages)

A Lenten Celebration

Lent offers a unique opportunity to celebrate the life, death, and resurrection of Jesus Christ. The following service may be used on Palm Sunday or at the conclusion of the death and dying unit.

To make this activity easier, make two copies of Lenten Celebration: one for you and the other to cut apart for the different student sections. The children should receive their reading parts the week before the celebration so they can practice and will feel comfortable with their participation.

Celebrating the Life, Death, and Resurrection of Jesus

OPENING SONG: Open this service with a song about Jesus. The children may sing together or listen to a record.

INTRODUCTION: "Today we remember the life, death, and resurrection of Jesus Christ. During his short life here on earth, Jesus taught us about his Father in heaven and showed us how to live a good life here on earth."

FIRST READER: "Jesus was born in a stable in Bethlehem almost two thousand years ago. His birth brought rejoicing to the heavens and to shepherds in the surrounding hills. Wise men followed his special star but others hardly noticed his birth."

SECOND READER: "Jesus gew up in Nazareth and was obedient to Mary and Joseph. When he was about thirty years old, Jesus began his public teaching. Jesus wanted everyone to know about his Father and how to live a kind and loving life here on earth."

TEACHER: "Let us share a quiet prayer together.

Jesus, you always shared your love with others. You showed us how to feed the hungry, take care of the sick, and visit the lonely. You told us to love all people as you did.

Now we will remember some of the people who knew Jesus."

MAN BORN BLIND: "Hello, I am the man who was born blind. It was very hard for me to earn a living. One day I met Jesus. He said, 'I am the Light of the World.' Before Jesus came into my life, my world was dark. Now I can see the faces of my mother and father. Now I can see the great joy that Jesus has brought into the world."

MARTHA: "I am Martha, the sister of Lazarus and Mary. Jesus was a good friend of our family. He often visited our home. One day, my brother Lazarus became very sick. Mary and I tried to reach Jesus, but before he got there my brother died and we buried his body. Jesus finally came and Mary and I ran to greet him. He told us, 'I am the resurrection and the life; if you believe in me, you shall never die!' Jesus went to Lazarus' tomb and brought him back to life. Jesus gave his life for others. He loved God very much. I am very grateful that Jesus is a part of my life."

LEPER: "Do you recognize me? I used to wear a bell and call out 'unclean' to everyone that came near. I had the terrible disease of leprosy. I could not visit my family or friends for fear they would catch it, too. I lived outside the town with the other lepers. It was a terrible life. One day Jesus of Nazareth came by. Ten of us went to ask Jesus for his help. Jesus said to us 'Go and show yourselves to the priests.' As we were walking down the road, an amazing thing happened! Our skin felt fresh and clean. The leprosy was gone. I hurried back to thank Jesus."

A FRIEND IN JERUSALEM: "I was standing on the side of the road and I watched as Jesus rode through the streets of Jerusalem. The whole city was in an uproar. A crowd of people spread their cloaks on the road. People were calling Jesus a king, but only a few days later the same crowd wanted to put him to death."

PETER: "I am Peter, a friend of Jesus. I was at the Last Supper. As a sign of service, Jesus washed the feet of all his Apostles. Then he broke the bread and shared the cup of wine. Jesus knew that he would soon die. He asked his friends to pray with him in the garden, but we were all tired and fell asleep. I woke when the soldiers came into the garden to arrest Jesus."

ROMAN SOLDIER: "I am a Roman soldier. I watched Jesus carry his cross through the streets of Jerusalem. I saw the pain in his eyes when he greeted his mother. I saw his anguish when he offered his life to God. This was truly a special man. I believe he was the Son of God."

TEACHER: "Let us take a quiet time to think about Jesus in our own lives. What could you tell others about him?" (Quiet time and sharing time—for those groups feeling comfortable about sharing their feelings and faith.)

THIRD READER: "Jesus taught us to take the time to pray. Let us say together the special prayer Jesus taught his apostles." (Recite the Lord's Prayer together.)

FOURTH READER: "Today we remember all the things Jesus did for us. Jesus died on the cross for all people. We believe that on the third day Jesus rose from the dead. He promised us the gift of everlasting life."

FIFTH READER: "As our celebration comes to a close, let us thank God for the gift of his son, Jesus. Jesus our Savior was born a baby like you and me. He taught us to see God's love in a new way and showed us the way to everlasting life. We have so much to celebrate this Easter season."

CLOSING SONG: "Long, Live God" from *Godspell* or another song of celebration.

a Time To LiVe, a Time To Die...

THIS BOOK ABOUT LIFE AND DEATH BELONGS TO:

_____

GOD Has Given me many special TaLenTS....

MY TaLenTS aRe:

WHEN I DIE, I WILL BE REMEMBERED AS A PERSON WHO LIKED:

FAVORITE PLACE

FAVORITE MOVIE

FAVORITE SONG

FAVORITE COLOR

FAVORITE FOOD

FAVORITE BOOK

FAVORITE T.V. SHOW

MY FEELINGS ABOUT DYING

WHAT MY FRIENDS WOULD MISS...

MY FEELINGS ABOUT DYING...

SOMETIMES I WORRY ABOUT...

WHAT I AM DOING TO HELP ME
LIVE A LONG LIFE...

LAST WILL and TESTAMENT

I,_____ BEING OF SOUND MIND and BODY, WISH
MY WORLDLY POSSESSIONS TO BE DIVIDED AS STATED:

_____

_____

_____

_____

_____

_____

_____

_____

WITNESS: _____ DATE: _____

WITNESS: _____ DATE: _____

EPITAPH

WHAT WOULD YOU LIKE ON YOUR TOMBSTONE? WHAT WOULD BE AN ACCURATE DESCRIPTION OF YOU AND YOUR LIFE IN A FEW SHORT WORDS?

HERE LIES:

_____

_____

_____

_____

_____

_____

_____

_____

HUNDREDS OF YEARS AFTER JESUS' DEATH HE IS STILL REMEMBERED

PLACE OF BIRTH:

THINGS HE DID WITH HIS FRIENDS:

STORIES HE TOLD US:

DAY OF HIS DEATH:

REMEMBERING JESUS

WHAT JESUS TOLD US ABOUT EVER-LASTING LIFE....

...IMPORTANT THINGS HE DID

HIS FAMILY

HIS FRIENDS...

Jesus carried
his cross
through the
streets of
Jerusalem.

I, too carry a cross. My cross is:

_____

_____

_____

_____

Simon helped
to carry the
cross of Jesus.
I, too, have
help incarry-
ing my cross.
My helpers are:

_____

_____

_____

_____

RESURRECTION SYMBOLS

CREATE YOUR OWN SYMBOL

MY SYMBOL HAS MEANING BECAUSE:

_____

_____

Reflection: Death and Dying

By _____

During the unit on death and dying I learned . . .

_____

_____

_____

_____

The part of the unit I liked best is_____

_____

The part of the unit I liked least is_____

_____

Death is_____

_____

We are called an "Alleluia People" because_____

_____

_____

**THANK YOU, JESUS, FOR YOUR DEATH
AND RESURRECTION!**

Closing Comments

Our gift of a school year is almost over and it's time for review and evaluation. Chapter Ten discusses peace and justice concepts for the end of the year. There is so much to do during the last class session. You want to spend some time reviewing major concepts studied. You need time to clean up and check in materials. You need time to say thank you to the people who deserve your thanks. The following activities help students review, say thanks, and encourage clean-up.

Dear God . . .
Another school year is almost over.
The children eagerly awaited in September
will soon leave us for summer play.
During our last few weeks together . . .
Help me to see the special gifts of each child.
Help me to see the wonder, delight, and pain
in their eyes as they grow
in the understandings
of our world.
Help me to emphasize the importance
of conserving our resources
and becoming educated consumers.
Help me to develop the importance
of nonviolent conflict resolution.
But, above all,
Help me to give all the children the self-confidence
to use their God-given gifts
for themselves,
for their families,
for their world community.
May you bless us all in our summer adventures.
Amen.

I think the biggest problem
facing my country is_____

_____ because

_____

_____

Peace-ing
the
Year
Together

Write the names of four people
who helped you this year.

_____

_____

_____

_____

NAME

_____

_____
is a famous *Peacemaker*
because_____

_____

My definition of *Peace* is:

_____

_____

_____

What did you like
best about this
class?_____

_____

Write a talent you shared with our
classroom community
this year._____

Write a talent you shared
this year:_____

_____

_____

Write the name of a famous black American.

_____

Name two countries where hunger is a big problem.

1._____

2._____

Call a person who might be lonely and would be cheered by your call.

I called:_____

Write the name of a famous woman. Why is she well-known?_____

_____

_____

Interview two people about how they handle conflict.
I talked to:

1._____

2._____

Thank five people who helped you this year. I thanked:

1._____

2._____

3._____

4._____

5._____

Why is world peace and brotherhood important?

_____

_____

_____

My definition of *Violence* is:_____

_____

_____

Name one "rip-off" commercial:

_____

_____

Please list five things you can do this summer to live the word *Christian*.

_____

_____

_____

List five things you can do this summer to help conserve resources:

1._____

2._____

3._____

4._____

5._____

Name one act of service you can do this summer:

_____

_____

135

FINISH

Evaluation:
Education for Peace and Justice

By _____

Why is education for peace so important?_____

_____

_____

What did you learn about yourself this year?_____

_____

_____

What did you learn about getting along with others?_____

_____

_____

What did you learn about problems facing the world?_____

_____

_____

What did you learn about world interdependence and
"Spaceship Earth"?_____

_____

_____

What is your role in promoting peace and justice?_____

_____

_____

AFTERWORD

The American Bishops have said to us, "To teach the ways of peace is not to weaken the nation's will, but to be concerned for the nation's soul."* Peace education is based on a concern for the soul and thus, is vital to our religious education curriculum. Peace education begins and ends with adults modeling respect, living community and solving problems nonviolently.

We have been given the gift of time. As Christian educators, we must teach children to value themselves and others and help them to view the earth as the home of the People of God. As Christian citizens, we must expect our political representatives to work for peace and our leaders to live justly and see justice as a global priority.

We have the time to make a difference. Peace education can help to make a difference. The choice belongs to us.

*"The Challenge of Peace"